BRAIN-BASED
Learning
With **Gifted**
Students

BRAIN-BASED Learning With Gifted Students

Lessons From Neuroscience on Cultivating Curiosity, Metacognition, Empathy, and Brain Plasticity

Kathryn Fishman-Weaver, Ph.D.

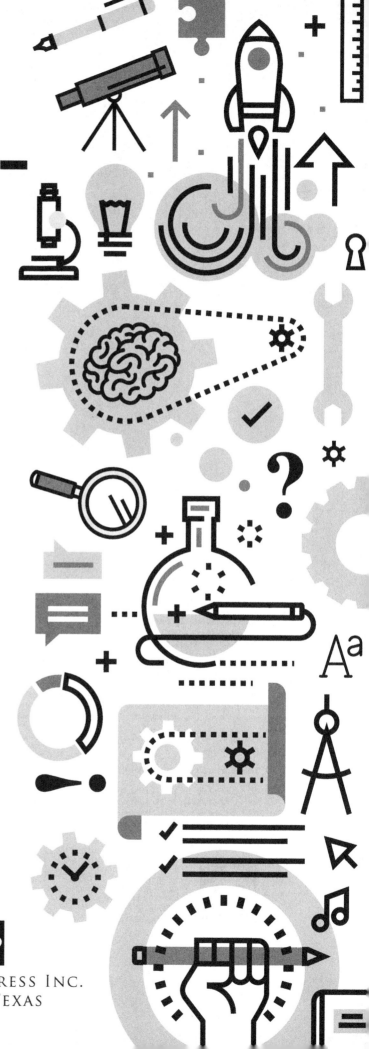

PRUFROCK PRESS INC.
WACO, TEXAS

Prufrock Press Inc.
P.O. Box 8813
Waco, TX 76714-8813
Phone: (800) 998-2208
Fax: (800) 240-0333
http://www.prufrock.com

Dedication

This book is dedicated to our future neuroscientists, cognitive psychologists, and science teachers, and also to all of the compassionate educators who encourage them along the way.

Table of Contents

Acknowledgments

Like all books, bringing this text to the world was a community effort. Knowing that acknowledgment lists are always incomplete, I want to particularly thank the following people who were instrumental in helping make this book possible.

Christopher Fishman-Weaver read the roughest of my rough drafts, kept me supplied in dark chocolate throughout the writing process, and continues to be my biggest fan.

Gifted education specialist Marilyn Toalson reviewed chapters of this book, and although her wise notes helped, her friendship and encouragement for this project helped me even more.

I reached out to several people in the science community, and all responded with encouragement. I owe a special shout-out to three in particular. Dr. David Beversdorf, Director of Graduate Studies in Neuroscience at the University of Missouri, helped me with much of the technical content of this book. His reviews strengthened my confidence in taking on this project and deepened my understanding about the brain. Likewise, Dr. Kerryane Monahan, a neurobiologist and award-winning science educator, graciously responded to my unsolicited tweet with interest in this project, smart notes and accuracy checks, and brain-based humor to keep me going. Pediatrician Dr. Lauren Miltenberg reviewed the health chapter for accuracy and guidance. I have long admired the Miltenberg family's commitment to youth health and deeply appreciated having Dr. Miltenberg's eyes on this project.

I had a beta-testing team of teachers and young scholars. Brian Stuhlman and his daughter Lilia (age 10), and Megan Lilien and her daughter Adelyn (age 10), sent me great comments and copies of their work on these activities. Brian and Megan have strong backgrounds in gifted and science education respectively, and their edits were always spot-on. Lilia's and Adelyn's honest suggestions and critiques absolutely made this book stronger.

Lilah Weaver (age 8) served as the lead beta tester for every student activity in this book. Like Lilia and Adelyn, she offered candid feedback on what worked and what didn't. Offended when I told her that she could help me with literature reviews when she was "a bit older," Lilah took it upon herself to survey the technical journals scattered across my desk and in the backseat of my car. She then submitted her own helpful summaries and diagrams to aid in my research process. Her triumphant "so there" when she presented these notes was apropos to the mission of this book—neuroscience is an appropriate and engaging topic of inquiry for elementary learners and teachers alike.

Stephanie McCauley and the wonderful people at Prufrock Press helped me nurture this fuzzy seed of an idea into the following comprehensive guide for students and educators. Prufrock Press continues to offer relevant and cutting-edge resources for neurodiverse learners, and I am proud to have this third title with them.

And finally, to you, my valued readers: May you find in these pages content to spark curiosity, engagement, and creativity.

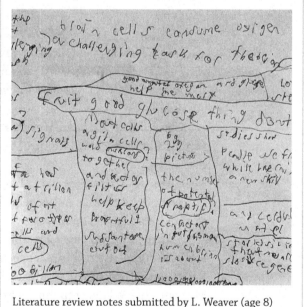

Literature review notes submitted by L. Weaver (age 8)

Introduction
Why Neuroscience?

In the last 25 years, researchers have made important discoveries about the brain. According to the National Institute of Neurological Disorders and Stroke (2020), "Scientists have learned more about the brain in the last 10 years than in all previous centuries because of the accelerating pace of research in neurological and behavioral science and the development of new research techniques" (para. 2). These discoveries directly matter for educators' work in the classroom. Knowing that "learning consists of reinforcing the connections between neurons" (Willis, 2006, p. 14), it behooves teachers to explore how this research on brain-based solutions might help better address students' complex learning needs. Neuroscientists working in the fields of learning and education explore how behaviors, thoughts, and feelings intersect with learning and how brain processes help or impede learning. Neuroscience and new work around neuroeducation have led to important advancements in understanding cognition, retention, memory, sensory processing, learning disabilities, emotional regulation, and giftedness. This information is vital for creating differentiated lessons that work in diverse classrooms. Further, learning about the brain is an empowering and relevant source of inquiry for both students and teachers.

There are many excellent resources on neuroscience, brain-based learning, and the nature and needs of gifted learners. What differentiates this book is its invitation for teachers to learn about neuroscience *with* their students. Actively

1

and intentionally including students as learners in this inquiry is a guiding force of the following chapters.

As a result of recent work around growth mindset (see especially Carol Dweck's [2006/2016] work), schools have learned more about neuroplasticity. Key takeaways include:

- when it comes to learning, process matters more than product;
- all brains continue to develop over time, and;
- educators can teach students to respond to challenges in ways that make them more able to solve complex problems both now and in the future.

Learning about mindset was transformative to classroom practices. As a school administrator and teacher, I have been struck by the power of teaching young people about neuroplasticity. When children learn that they can become more adept at working through challenges, they become more open to challenge and more confident in their approaches to learning. Understanding how learning happens makes for better learners. As I watched this happen in classroom after classroom, I started to wonder how teaching students about their brains might lead to cognitively healthy and more engaged classrooms.

KEY CONCEPT

Neuroplasticity: The ability of the brain to reorganize (and grow) synaptic connections.

When students learn about cardiovascular health, they make choices that are healthier for their hearts and circulatory system. When they join an athletic team, coaches teach them the rules of the game and also how their muscles work and can grow stronger. *Brain-Based Learning With Gifted Students* offers similar research-based information for educators and students to explore how learning happens and how they can become more adept learners. Understanding how the brain works is a relevant and engaging topic of inquiry for the gifted education classroom.

Lessons from neuroscience give teachers a platform to better understand the particularities of giftedness, including asynchrony, affective development, emotional regulation, and talent development. This field also provides compelling interdisciplinary language to help students understand their unique brains. Imaging technology and research continue to show that the human brain is complex and individualized. Yeh and colleagues (2016) at Carnegie Melon used imaging technology to show that (1) every human brain is unique, (2) connections are very plastic, and (3) researchers can chart some changes in the brain due to social and environmental factors. They stated, "The specific brain characteristics that define an individual are encoded by the unique pattern of connections between the billions of neurons in the brain" (para. 1). In the words of neuroscientist Nicole Tetreault (2019), the brain is "as distinctive as a fingerprint" (para. 2). It is important and empowering for children to know that their brains are unique, special, and constantly developing over their lifetime.

How to Use This Book

Each chapter is organized around a specific neuroscience concept for educators and their students to explore together. This book is not a scripted curriculum; instead it provides research-based information and engagement opportunities aligned with big ideas in science. The activities and lessons in this book give students an opportunity to learn about neuroscience within the context of understanding and caring for their unique brains and those in their communities.

The chapters include three distinct sections:

- A clear and concise research overview on why this concept works and matters. The research rationale gives educators important background information for the unit of study.
- Specific activities and reproducibles for teaching this concept in your classroom. Each set of activities concludes with a synthesizing "make it stick" project.
- Extension ideas and transfer notes. These are ways to stretch and deepen these activities based on the unique interests and needs of your students. This section includes a discussion of how to apply this brain-based concept to other content areas.

Big Ideas in Science

The Next Generation Science Standards (NGSS Lead States, 2013) identify a set of crosscutting concepts that connect scientific domains. Calling out crosscutting concepts helps students understand the interrelating knowledge between science fields as students build a worldview of observing and understanding phenomena scientifically. This book focuses students' (and teachers') attention on five Big Ideas in Science informed by the NGSS. These include: Patterns, Cause and Effect, Structure and Function, Stability and Change, and Interdependence.

Eight Essential Concepts

There are eight key neuroscience concepts in this book:
- **Concept 1:** Brain Anatomy 101
- **Concept 2:** Interrogative Inquiry
- **Concept 3:** Maximizing Metacognitive Moments
- **Concept 4:** Sparking Connection With Wonder
- **Concept 5:** Social Cognition
- **Concept 6:** Neuroplasticity
- **Concept 7:** Emotional Regulation
- **Concept 8:** Keeping the Brain Healthy

Although I was purposeful in designing a scope and sequence, I know readers may have different pressing needs in their classroom. For example, you might need background information and activities on social cognition right now. If so, start there and then return to the beginning and work through the units as intended with your students.

Gifted Programming Standards

The chapters in this book are presented for inquiry with gifted students. All activities are aligned to the updated National Association of Gifted Children (NAGC, 2019) Pre-K–Grade 12 Gifted Programming Standards. A chart listing the standards addressed in each chapter can be found in the NAGC Programming Standards Alignment at the end of the book.

A Few Introductory Notes

Brain-Based Learning

Whenever teachers engage students in learning, problem solving, critical thinking, or connecting their thoughts, feelings, and behaviors, they are also engaging the brain. Learning and the brain are integrally connected. Although classrooms are learning-rich spaces, are they brain-based spaces?

How much do educators know about the brain? How much professional development do teachers receive on cognition, affect, and neuroscience? Are teachers engaging in brain-based learning by chance, or are they building their practices on a body of well-vetted research about the brain? Classroom communities are deeply invested in learning, memory, emotional regulation, and decision making; therefore it makes sense for both students and teachers to know more about how this process happens in the brain.

I encourage educators to think of this as the intersection between brain science and classroom practice. In the last 10 years, brain-based learning has gained popularity as a high-interest topic for educators seeking to better understand and serve the diverse learners in their classrooms. Brain-based learning refers to instructional strategies grounded in the neuroscience of learning. Although teachers engage the brain whether or not they have in-depth knowledge of brain processes, won't they engage students more effectively if they know more about how the brain functions and processes information? Those working in neuroeducation believe this is a worthy hypothesis. Throughout the following chapters, I invite you to test this hypothesis in your school community.

Democratizing Neuroscience

Embarking on this project sent me into a notable spiral of imposter syndrome. Before anyone found out I was working on such a project, I wanted to be sure that I could answer any question that might come up about the amygdala, hippocampus, or frontal cortex. I dove into highly technical texts on neurology, neuroscience, and neuroeducation. I took detailed notes and quizzed myself on the function of the thalamus, the occipital lobe, and reticular activating system.

My fascination with the brain wasn't new. Diagnosed with chronic migraines as a toddler and identified as gifted in elementary school, I have long been interested in understanding both the brain at large as well as the particular functions of my own unique brain. In first grade I brought in an MRI scan of my brain for show-and-tell and then gave a presentation on magnetic imaging. During my graduate program in special education, I studied cognition as it related to learning disabilities and differences. My Ph.D. research explored the affective domain. All of this is to say: I had valid reasons for proposing this project, so why the hesitation to tell others?

I knew just enough about the brain to know how little I knew, and I was worried about being found out for my limitations. As professionals, we must stop doing this to ourselves. Although I certainly don't have the same understanding of brain function that a neurologist or neuroscientist has, my experiences with how brain-based research impacts teaching and learning offers a valuable perspective for classroom practice. In fact, educators are among the best-suited professionals to shed light on how neuroscience can be translated to the classroom.

Teachers, particularly teachers of students who learn differently, including those in gifted programs and special education services, need and deserve access to the latest research in neuroscience. Given their professional work, these educators also have experiences and questions that could push brain-based research forward in new and exciting ways. Just as a teacher can appreciate a journal about a memory study, a neuroscientist can appreciate an academic paper on reading development. In fact, in both of these examples, cross-disciplinary connections strengthen what the reader brings to these texts. In this highly connected world, this book is, in part, a call to cultivate interdisciplinary conversations about the brain and learning.

It is my great hope that *Brain Based Learning With Gifted Students* sparks this same joy for discovery and exploration in your own classrooms, schools, and districts.

KEY TERMS FOR EDUCATORS

- **Brain-based learning:** Instructional strategies grounded in the neuroscience of learning; the intersection between brain science and classroom practice.

- **Growth mindset:** Dweck's (2006/2016) applied theory on achievement and learning based on nurturing persistence and process while celebrating challenge and resilience.

- **National Association for Gifted Children (NAGC):** National organization with strong state-level connection focused on education, advocacy, community building, and research around supporting gifted and talented students and educators working with these populations.

- **Neuroeducation:** A division of neuroscience focused on brain processes that help or impede learning, cognition, retention, memory, sensory processing, learning disabilities, emotional regulation, and giftedness.

- **Neuroscience:** Interdisciplinary field of science studying the brain.

Chapter 1

Brain Anatomy 101

ESSENTIAL QUESTION

- How can learning about the key structures of the human brain help you become a better learner?

BIG IDEAS IN SCIENCE

- Structure and Function
- Interdependence

Brain-Based Teaching and Learning Requires Knowledge About the Brain

Despite all of my years of schooling, I had very few formal lessons on the anatomical features of the human brain. My high school and college biology classes briefly covered brain function as it relates to the central nervous system. However, they didn't dive into any of the specific or unique features of the human brain. My psychology classes covered development broadly, often reminding me that my prefrontal cortex (PFC) would not be fully developed until ages 25–28. Other than my not-yet-fully-rational PFC, the brain as an object of study was largely missing from the classes I took in my teens and early 20s. This seems like an important missed opportunity.

A lot has changed since I took high school science. The addition of dynamic courses such as AP Anatomy and Physiology, AP Psychology, and Project Lead the Way (PLTW) Biomedical Science give high school students more access to learning about the brain. Although these courses are excellent, many rural and urban students continue to have limited access to them. Further, these are also seen as high school-level topics, meaning it is uncommon to find similar units or lessons in the elementary classroom. And yet, elementary students hear about brain research on TV, podcasts, magazines, etc., and sometimes come to class wanting to talk about it. When they pose questions on these topics, are teachers equipped with the knowledge to answer them? Do teachers have the background information to recognize a *neuromyth* propagated in the media and to call it out? Do teacher preparation programs include lessons that can help teachers answer general questions on brain anatomy and function?

KEY CONCEPT

Neuromyth: A frequently referenced, but false, belief about how the brain functions (e.g., right brain and left brain).

When I progressed through my master's and Ph.D. programs (specifically in teaching and learning fields), my classes continued to discuss the brain only in reference to disorders, disabilities, and dysfunctions. Even these lessons occurred somewhat abstractly from the neurological processes of what was (or wasn't) happening within the brain. It felt as though my colleagues and professors regarded the brain as mysterious and complex, much like a distant galaxy or the inner workings of a black hole. Although the brain is complex and mysterious, this complexity shouldn't preclude anyone from studying it. Just as astrophysicists have learned more about gravitational acceleration inside a black hole, neuroscientists have also made important advancements in understanding the mysteries of the human brain. This new understanding has the potential to improve teaching practices, and yet educators have limited exposure to brain-based research as it applies to the profession. This absence of scientific information perpetuates neuromyths, misunderstanding, and possibly even some poor decisions.

According to a recent report by the Online Learning Consortium:

> Educators make countless decisions about their teaching and course design that are likely to impact on how well their students learn. At the heart of these decisions is a set of ideas about how learning proceeds, so it is self-evidently important that these ideas are valid and reflect our current scientific understanding. *And yet, a growing body of research is revealing that many of the underlying beliefs of educators about learning are based on myth and misunderstanding—particularly in regard to the brain* [emphasis added]. (Howard-Jones, 2019, p. 4)

Although this report was prepared at the higher education level, the premise can be extrapolated to K–12. In fact, elementary schools' distance from the research epicenters of higher education may put them at an even greater risk for perpetuating neuromyths.

Contextualizing Giftedness in the Brain

Most professionals agree that giftedness is contextualized in the brain—meaning that gifted students learn and process differently than their age-level peers. This section summarizes some of the major findings and hypotheses from the brain-based research on giftedness and then shares a sociological caution as researchers design future studies on giftedness and the brain.

A study by the UCLA Brain Mapping Institute followed more than 300 children for 12 years, mapping brain development (Tetreault, 2019). Working with high-IQ children, researchers produced 3-D models that illustrated asynchronous brain development, meaning that regions of the brain grew at varying rates and were person-dependent, not time-dependent. Repeated studies have shown that gifted individuals have a more activated right prefrontal cortex, enhanced cerebral bilateralism, and neural processing patterns often characterized as more complex (meaning more parts of the brain are working together during complex tasks) and more efficient (meaning less brain activity is required for similar tasks; Mrazik & Dombrowski, 2010).

Tasks, Talents, and Processing Speed. Functional magnetic resonance imaging (fMRI) studies often look at how individuals respond to specific tasks. When someone has a high ability at the task, their neural processes will be different than someone with an average ability at the task and/or someone who struggles with the task. Studies that account for ability, such as Rypma et al.'s (2006) study on performance speed, show that if someone has a high ability in the task, then their processing may occur in a different lobe. In Hoppe and Stojanovic's (2009) study, subjects were grouped according to processing speed on a common numeracy task: "While the fast-reacting subjects showed posterior (i.e. parietal) brain activation during the task, the slower-reacting subjects showed anterior (i.e. frontal) activation during the identical task" (para. 4). Whether the processing is more complex (using more regions of the brain) or more efficient (less brain activation) is task-dependent. Gifted students are not equally advanced across all tasks. For the tasks in which they exhibit a high ability, fMRI scans suggest that gifted and high-ability individuals may exhibit neural efficiency, meaning they require less brain activity to complete the task (Dunst et al., 2014).

Increased Bilateralism. In O'Boyle's (2008) work with mathematically gifted children and brain development, he noted:

> Math-gifted children exhibit signs of enhanced right-hemisphere development, and when engaged in the thinking process, tend to rely on mental imagery. They further manifest heightened interhemispheric exchange of information between the left and right sides of the brain, reflecting an unusual degree of neural connectivity. (p. 181)

These increased bilateral connections allow for "enhanced interhemispheric communication" (Munro, 2013). This means that information is processed, coordinated, and integrated differently in gifted students' ability areas. These connections are facilitated by the *corpus callosum*, the thick band of nerve fibers between the right and left hemispheres of the cerebral cortex.

Frontoparietal Network. Although there are many distinctions that make each brain unique, researchers have found that the most significant differences are often found in the *frontoparietal network*, the system that connects the frontal and parietal lobes. The frontoparietal network helps individuals make quick decisions about how to respond or behave in various situations. Gifted students tend to show greater activation across the frontoparietal network than their nongifted peers.

Although there is excellent research to draw on, there are still many unanswered questions about what exactly giftedness looks like in the brain. Neuroscientists like Tetreault and others, who have a specific background in giftedness, are currently helping to move this research forward. This is an exciting area for future studies in neuroscience, but it should be pursued with caution.

The ways subjects are identified for these neurobiological studies and the ways students are identified for gifted programs often reveal a central equity issue. Most states and districts use a version of a general intelligence test as part (or all) of their identification process. Although there is some variation state to state, an IQ ≥ 130 (97th percentile) is often considered a standard metric for identifying giftedness. IQ tests are limited in what they reveal about general processing and also biased in whom they identify. Therefore, NAGC (n.d.-a) recommended against using this (or any) single instrument to determine giftedness, as it is "estimated that African American, Hispanic American, and Native American students are underrepresented by at least 50% in programs for the gifted" (para. 3).

As neurobiological studies on gifted youth expand, researchers must be well-versed in the issues surrounding equity and gifted identification so that they control for the material privileges higher socioeconomic status affords (e.g., excellent nutrition, access to healthcare, and cultural capital). Without this framework, new studies on giftedness would have complicated utility at best and, at worst, could be potentially divisive to work on equity in gifted education.

Learning With Students

This book asks you to engage in inquiry *with* your students. If your formal education was similar to mine, brain anatomy may be relatively new to you, too. Spend extra time with the material ahead of teaching it. Use the memory jogs I wrote for students, such as *Flamingos Pounce on Trampolines* (to remember the order of the four lobes of the brain). Gather materials that will help the lesson come alive (e.g., walnuts, pillowcases, clay, paint, swim caps, etc.). You may have to make some adjustments to pacing, particularly for younger students, to support them with the new technical vocabulary in this chapter.

KEY TERMS FOR EDUCATORS

- **Brainstem:** A small but important section of the mid- and hind-brain that controls the flow of messages between the brain and the rest of the body, as well as vital functions including breathing, swallowing, heart rate, blood pressure, consciousness, and sleep/wake.

- **Cerebral cortex:** The outer, wrinkled "gray-matter" layer of the cerebrum, divided into two hemispheres (left and right); the most advanced structure of the brain, where higher order thinking, reasoning, learning, perceiving, and memory happen.

- **Cerebrum:** The largest and uppermost part of the brain; accounts for two-thirds of the total weight of the brain.

- **Frontal lobe:** Supports cognitive tasks (e.g., problem solving), emotional control, and voluntary movement; the prefrontal cortex is part of the frontal lobe (see *prefrontal cortex*).

- **Frontoparietal network:** The system that connects the frontal and parietal lobes, this network helps individuals make quick decisions about how to respond or behave in various situations.

- **Functional magnetic resonance imaging (fMRI):** A noninvasive procedure that produces pictures of the metabolic function of the human brain; measures activation areas of the brain in response to sensory stimuli (sight, touch, taste, smell, problem solving); often used by neuroscientists for brain-mapping research.

- **Occipital lobe:** Manages sight and visual processes.

- **Parietal lobe:** Supports spatial orientation and processing of the environment, including sensations such as temperature, taste, touch, and movement.

- **Prefrontal cortex (PFC):** A large region at the front of the frontal lobe involved in higher order thinking tasks, including planning, decision making, social behavior, and personality; the last region in the brain to fully develop.

- **Temporal lobe:** Manages and connects memories to senses, allowing individuals to recognize language, music, etc.

Classroom Application

Unit Overview

This is a high-level overview on the anatomy of the human brain. Students begin by learning that just as no two snowflakes or fingerprints are alike, each brain is also uniquely wired. fMRI scans have enabled researchers to refine knowledge of brain regions through advanced blood flow images illuminating neural connections. Students should know that although the brain is complex, it is also an appropriate and exciting object of study. Students should also know that their individual brains make them unique. Although all people share certain neurobiological traits, no one else has exactly the same constellation of thoughts, feelings, and processes. Many different kinds of thinkers and brains are needed to move the world forward—each of the young people in your classrooms is uniquely suited to offer a slightly nuanced perspective and experience.

The unit moves into an exploration of three major divisions of the brain (the forebrain, midbrain, and hindbrain), the two hemispheres of the cerebral cortex, and the four lobes of each hemisphere.

KEY CONCEPTS

- **Forebrain, midbrain, hindbrain:** These are the three main structures of the brain (see Figure 1). Eighty-five percent of the brain is found in the forebrain. Although most of the lessons in this book relate to this structure, the activities spend some time teaching about the brainstem (the top part is located in the midbrain and the rest is located in the hindbrain). The brainstem controls several vital functions, including breathing, swallowing, heart rate, blood pressure, consciousness, and sleep/wake, and allows the brain to communicate with the body.
- **Hemispheres and lobes:** The cerebral cortex is divided into two *hemispheres*. The left hemisphere helps control the right side of the body, and the right hemisphere helps control the left side of the body. The two hemispheres are connected by the *corpus callosum*, which runs down the middle of the brain. (*Note.* The idea of students being either left brained or right brained is a

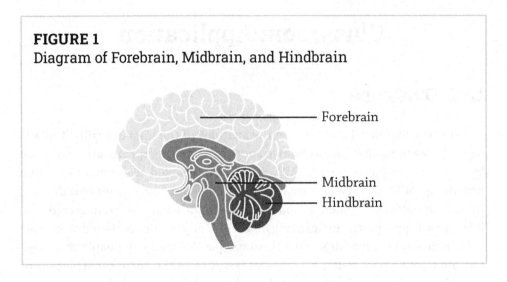

FIGURE 1
Diagram of Forebrain, Midbrain, and Hindbrain

Forebrain

Midbrain

Hindbrain

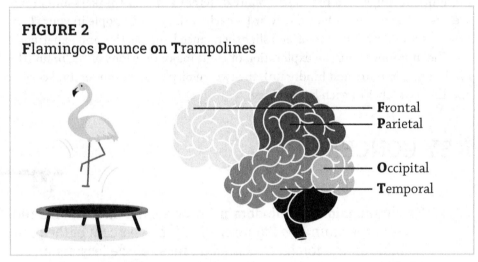

FIGURE 2
Flamingos Pounce on Trampolines

Frontal

Parietal

Occipital

Temporal

myth. Do not perpetuate this neuromyth in your classrooms.) The two hemispheres work together to perform both logical and creative tasks. The cerebral cortex is further divided into four sections called *lobes.* These are the frontal, parietal, occipital, and temporal. Use the funny mnemonic *Flamingos Pounce on Trampolines* to remember the order and location of the lobes (see Figure 2).

Students synthesize these concepts by making diagrams of the brain. I have provided several suggestions for materials they can use for their diagrams from the simple (a poster with standard art materials) to the complex (different colored play dough and clay) to the silly (wearable swim cap diagrams; this idea comes from the biomedical science course from Project Lead the Way—see https://www.pltw.org/our-programs/pltw-biomedical-science). Directions with the structures for students to include in their diagrams can be found in the "make it stick" section of this unit.

Time Suggestions

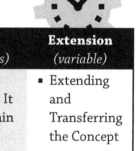

Class 1 (15 minutes)	Class 2 (30 minutes)	Class 3 (20 minutes)	Class 4 (30 minutes)	Extension (variable)
• Handout 1.1: Your Brain Is Uniquely Yours • Essential Question and Learning Objectives	• Handout 1.2: Structures of the Brain • Handout 1.3: The Walnut and the Pillowcase: Two Connected Halves	• Handout 1.4: The Four Lobes of the Human Brain	• Handout 1.5: Make It Stick!: Brain Diagrams	• Extending and Transferring the Concept

STUDENT ACTIVITIES
Brain Anatomy 101

LET'S INVESTIGATE

Essential Question

- How can learning about the key structures of the human brain help you become a better learner?

Learning Objectives

By the end of this unit, I will . . .
- think critically about how my brain is uniquely wired;
- identify the cerebral cortex, right and left hemispheres, and four lobes of the human brain;
- debunk the right and left brain neuromyth;
- explain the function of each of the four lobes of the human brain; and
- create a diagram of the human brain.

Brain Anatomy 101

Name: _____ Date: _____

HANDOUT 1.1
Your Brain Is Uniquely Yours

Have you ever heard that no two snowflakes are exactly alike? Do you think that is true? Snowflakes seem pretty similar. It turns out that the closer you look, the less similar they might be. If you examine snowflakes at the **molecular** level, then no two snowflakes are exactly alike.

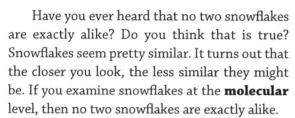

> **KEY TERM**
>
> **Molecular** means at the level of the molecule. A molecule is the smallest particle of a chemical compound. Although molecules are extremely small, atoms are even smaller; that is because atoms make up molecules.

According to snow scientist Charles Knight, each snow crystal contains approximately 10 quintillion or 10,000,000,000,000,000,000 water molecules (Helmenstine, 2020). Think about all of the different ways those molecules can arrange and rearrange themselves! Because of this variation, each snowflake is unique from every other.

Just as no two snowflakes are exactly alike, neither are two sets of fingerprints. Your unique fingerprints were likely formed 3 months *before* you were born. Although your fingers grow throughout childhood and adolescence, your unique fingerprint pattern is the same one that was formed before your birth. So how was it made? There are many variables that affect the unique formation of fingerprints. These include the oxygen levels in the blood while you were developing, the prenatal nutrition you had access to, the way you were positioned, and how the amniotic fluid was swirling around you. Those are several factors that led to that particular pattern you see on your thumb.

Given that every snowflake is unique, and every fingerprint is unique, do you think the same is true about your brain? Is your brain uniquely distinct from anyone else's brain? By this point, it won't surprise you to learn that it is.

In recent years, researchers have used **Functional MRI** or **fMRI** to identify the neural connections in our brains. An fMRI uses a strong magnetic field and radio waves to create detailed pictures of blood flow to the brain. By analyzing these images, researchers have learned that our brains vary from each other in much the same way our fingerprints do (Finn et al., 2015).

In other words, your brain both makes you unique and is uniquely yours! There is no other brain that thinks, responds, processes, and makes connections in exactly the same way yours does.

References

Finn, E. S., Shen, X., Scheinost, D., Rosenberg, M. D., Huang, J., Chun, M. M., & Constable, R. T. (2015). Functional connectome fingerprinting: Identifying individuals using patterns of brain connectivity. *Nature Neuroscience, 18*(11), 1664–1671. https://doi.org/10.1038/nn.4135

Helmenstine, A. M. (2020). *No two snowflakes alike—true or false*. ThoughtCo. https://www. thoughtco.com/why-all-snowflakes-are-different-609167

Brain Anatomy 101

HANDOUT 1.1, *continued*

Comprehension and Reflection Questions

1. This article covered several different topics. What surprised you the most in this reading?

   _____

   _____

   _____

   _____

2. How are snowflakes, fingerprints, and human brains similar? _____

   _____

   _____

   _____

3. What are molecules made of? _____

   _____

   _____

   _____

4. Name three factors that can impact what your fingerprints look like:

   a. _____

   b. _____

   c. _____

4. What technology do researchers use to study the neural connections in the brain?

   _____

   _____

   _____

   _____

5. If you were to summarize this article with one thematic word, what word would you choose?

   _____

Brain Anatomy 101

Name: _____ Date: _____

HANDOUT 1.2

Structures of the Brain

In order to better understand the complex brain, we will break it down to its parts. First, let's learn about the three major structures of the brain: the forebrain, the midbrain, and the hindbrain.

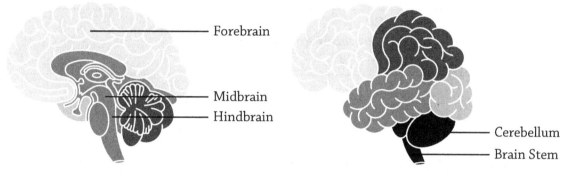

The **forebrain** is responsible for thinking, perceiving, producing and understanding language, receiving and processing sensory information, and controlling motor functions. The forebrain is the most advanced structure of the brain and also the biggest, making up about 85% of the human brain. In most lessons, this is the part of the brain that we will focus on.

The **midbrain** connects the forebrain and hindbrain. It contains the upper brain stem and is responsible for voluntary movement, eye movement, seeing depth, initial processing sounds, and some of your reflexes. The **brain stem** manages messages between the brain and the rest of the body. It controls breathing, swallowing, heart rate, blood pressure, consciousness, and whether you are awake or asleep. The top part of the brain stem is part of the midbrain, and the rest of the brain stem is located in the hindbrain.

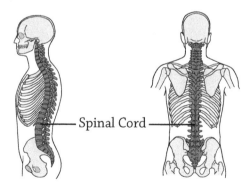

Although small, the **hindbrain** still includes some very important features, such as most of the brain stem, the top of the spinal cord, and the cerebellum.

- The **spinal cord** connects the brain and the nervous system. It is protected by a bony spinal column made up of bones called vertebrae.
- The **cerebellum** helps with posture, balance, coordination, and speech.

These structures work together to coordinate responses and functions throughout the body.

Brain Anatomy 101

HANDOUT 1.2, *continued*

Comprehension and Reflection Questions

1. What surprised you in learning about the structures of the brain?

   _____

   _____

2. What are the three major structures of the brain?

   a. _____

   b. _____

   c. _____

4. Name three functions of the brain stem.

   a. _____

   b. _____

   c. _____

5. What structure is responsible for voluntary movement, eye movement, seeing depth, processing sounds, and some of your reflexes?

   _____

6. What is the most advanced structure of the brain and also the biggest?

   _____

7. What structure includes most of the brain stem, the top of the spinal cord, and the cerebellum?

   _____

8. What are the bones in the spinal cord called?

   _____

9. Recognizing that they are all important, which structure do you think is most important and why?

   _____

   _____

Brain Anatomy 101

HANDOUT 1.3

The Walnut and the Pillowcase: Two Connected Halves

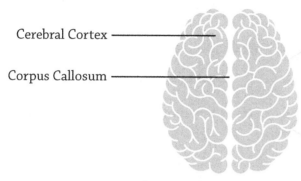

Cerebral Cortex

Corpus Callosum

Left Hemisphere   Right Hemisphere

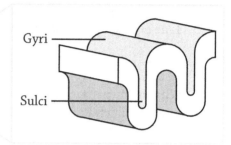

Gyri

Sulci

The **cerebral cortex** is the outermost layer of the forebrain. It is the bumpy, walnut-like surface that comes to mind when you think of the human brain.

The cerebral cortex is divided into two **hemispheres**. The left hemisphere helps control the right side of the body, and the right hemisphere helps control the left side of the body. The two hemispheres are connected by a thick band of nerve fibers called the **corpus callosum**, which runs down the middle of the brain. The corpus callosum is the largest white matter structure in the human brain. White matter is brain tissue made of nerve fibers. These fibers are covered with a type of fat called myelin, which gives white matter its white color.

Why Is the Human Brain So Wrinkly?

The human brain has ridges called **gyri** and crevices called **sulci**, which increase its surface area and processing power. Imagine you had a pillowcase and you smoothed it out flat. Now imagine you took that same pillowcase and crumpled it up into a ball. You would still have the same pillowcase, right? This is a pretty good comparison for the brain; in fact, if you smoothed out the human brain, it would be about as large as a pillowcase!

NEUROMYTH BUSTED

Have you ever heard that people are either *right brained* (to mean creative) or *left brained* (to mean logical)? This is false!

Takeaway Fact: The two halves of your connected brain work together to help you function, process, and feel. Although the two hemispheres do have some unique structures, neuroscientists have shown that both hemispheres are important for creative and logical tasks. In other words, we use both hemispheres, or one connected brain.

Brain Anatomy 101

Name: _____ Date: _____

Comprehension and Reflection Questions

1. How many hemispheres are in the human brain?

   _____

2. True or false: The right hemisphere helps control the left side of the body.

   _____

3. What is the name of the large band of nerve fibers that connect the hemispheres? Label it on the illustration on the previous page.

   _____

4. True or false: The right brain is responsible for creativity. Defend your answer.

   _____

   _____

   _____

   _____

5. How do gyri and sulci give the brain more surface area?

   _____

   _____

   _____

   _____

HANDOUT 1.4

The Four Lobes of the Human Brain

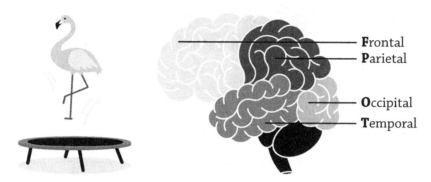

- **F**rontal
- **P**arietal
- **O**ccipital
- **T**emporal

The cerebral cortex is further divided into four sections called **lobes**. These are the: frontal, parietal, occipital, and temporal. You can use the funny mnemonic **Flamingos Pounce on Trampolines** to help you remember the order of these lobes, beginning clockwise from the front.

Frontal Lobe	**P**arietal Lobe

Responsible for logic, reasoning, organization, and emotional control/regulation.	Responsible for spatial orientation and processing sensations, such as touch, temperature, and pain.
Occipital Lobe	**T**emporal Lobe

Responsible for visual processing to identify objects and determine depth, distance, and location.	Responsible for processing information, such as sound, language, and memory.

Brain Anatomy 101

Name: _____   Date: _____

Comprehension and Reflection Questions

Name the Lobe

1. This, the smallest lobe in the human brain, helps you recognize your friends and determine how far away something is.

   _____

2. Ouch. If it wasn't for this lobe, you might leave your hand on a hot stove and burn yourself.

   _____

3. When you are feeling big emotions like anger, elation, or exasperation, you can be pretty sure a lot is happening in this lobe.

   _____

4. One day at choir practice, Malia's mother called. Malia answered the phone and switched from English to Swahili and then back to English. This lobe helped her with both the language and music processing.

   _____

Label the Lobes of the Brain

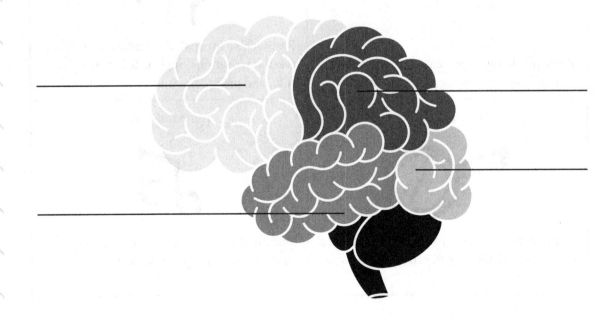

Name: _____ Date: _____

Make It Stick!: Brain Diagrams

1. You have **ONE** connected and unique brain that is distinct from all other brains—past, present, and future.
2. The human brain is divided into **TWO** hemispheres (right and left).
3. There are **THREE** major structures of the brain: forebrain, midbrain, and hindbrain.
4. Both hemispheres are further divided into **FOUR** lobes: the frontal, parietal, temporal, and occipital. (*Hint:* Remember the mnemonic **Flamingos Pounce on Trampolines**.)

Challenge

Diagram the human brain, using one of the following three options:
- **Swim Cap Brain:** Create your diagram on a plain white swim cap.
- **Sculpt a Brain:** Using colored clay or playdough, sculpt a 3-D model of the brain.
- **Big Brain Poster:** Using paints or colored pencils, create a large poster illustrating the different parts of the brain.

Your diagram should include as many of the following structures as possible:

The forebrain	Gyri and sulci
The midbrain	Corpus callosum
The hindbrain	The frontal lobe
Brain stem	The parietal lobe
Spinal cord	The temporal lobe
Right hemisphere	The occipital lobe
Left hemisphere	

Extending and Transferring the Concept

The activities in this unit offer an entry point for exploring brain anatomy and learning concepts. The following are additional ideas to extend these activities in your classroom.

Handout 1.1: Your Brain Is Uniquely Yours

- **Learn about MRI and fMRI:** The references to atoms, MRI, and fRMI can be an excellent springboard for additional research. Possible research prompts/questions include:
  - What are the different parts of the atom, and how are those affected by magnetic resonance?
  - Compare and contrast MRI and fMRI. How are the images produced by these two different, and what can they tell us?

- **Summary justification:** One of the comprehension questions asks students to summarize the key point of this article. Given the many topics covered in the article, this is a great opportunity to talk about context and justification—key skills students need as they tackle nonfiction texts.

Handout 1.2: Structures of the Brain

- **Compare and contrast the human brain with the brains of other mammals and animals:** Divide your students into research groups, with each group reporting on one of the following questions. You could also keep these research questions available at an extension center for students to explore during independent work time.
  - What brain structures do we find in all (or most) mammals?
  - How is the human brain unique from that of other animals?
  - What might account for the similarities between brain structures across animals?
  - Which animal has a brain structure most similar to the human brain? What are the key similarities and differences?
  - Do all animals have a brain? Why or why not?

Handout 1.3: The Walnut and the Pillowcase: *Two Connected Halves*

- **Pillowcase demonstration:** Surface area and size are challenging concepts to visualize. Make them more tactile by bringing in pillowcases for students to scrunch up and flatten out. This will help with comprehension.
- **Parachute demonstration:** Working together as a class, use a parachute to create a giant brain demonstration of the structures introduced in this activity.
  - First, scrunch the parachute together tightly. Next, have everyone grab onto the edge, inflate the parachute in the air, and sit down on their edge. Ask students what this demonstrates about surface area and how it connects to what they have learned about the brain.
  - Ask students if they can demonstrate the corpus callosum and divide the inflated parachute into two hemispheres. (*Note.* This will likely take multiple attempts and a lot of collaboration.)
  - If students complete the corpus callosum challenge, ask them to work together to demonstrate gyri and sulci.

Handout 1.4: The Four Lobes of the Human Brain

- **Create your own "name the lobe" questions:** This handout includes one scenario for each of the lobes. Students can work in small groups to create additional scenarios. Have students write their scenario on one side of an index card and their answer and rationale on another. Place all index cards in a hat or basket and draw them out one at a time for a classwide game.
- **All about a lobe:** Divide students into four expert groups and assign each one of the lobes—frontal, parietal, occipital, or temporal—for further research. Students can work through a short neuroscience or medical article on the latest research about this lobe and practice close reading and summarizing strategies for nonfiction. I recommend identifying these articles in advance for younger students. After students have researched and summarized their findings, do a jigsaw activity where groups are reassembled with one representative from each of the expert teams. This way all students have a chance to teach others about their research and learn more about all four lobes.
- **Learn about the frontoparietal network:** Figure 3 is an example of a quick reading you can share with your students.

> **FIGURE 3**
> Frontoparietal Network Reading
>
> #### Act Fast!: What Does the Frontoparietal Network Do?
>
> Although there are many distinctions that make your brain uniquely yours, researchers have found that the most significant differences are usually found in the **frontoparietal network**. This is the system that connects the frontal and parietal lobes. It helps you make quick decisions about how to respond or behave in various situations. The next time you and your sibling respond differently to being asked to set the table, or to winning a soccer game, or to accidently burning the chocolate chip cookies, know that part of these differences rests in the frontoparietal network.

- **Have fun with mnemonics:** Why do mnemonics work? They help students organize information into different connections and cues for easier retrieval. Chapter 4 will explore more about sparking connections in the brain. Until then, teach students some more helpful mnemonics (e.g., *My Very Excellent Mother Just Served Us Nachos* to help remember the planets in order from the sun) and then have students develop their own.

Handout 1.5: Make It Stick!: *Brain Diagrams*

- **Brain lab:** Invite families and school community members to a showcase of your brain diagrams. At the showcase, make sure students can identify and explain the structures of the brain they have included in their diagrams. You can even include a work table in your classroom for students to help guests create their own brain diagram.

Additional Extensions

The brain should become an ongoing topic of inquiry in classroom conversations. Transfer this objective across classes and units by encouraging students to talk about what is happening in their brains as they work on complex problems, master new skills, process emotions, listen to music, and explore stimuli. What structures are facilitating these activities and processes? Set norms to ensure these conversations are both strength-based and research-informed. Other extensions include:

- **Extension centers:** Set up extension centers in your classroom with research questions to foster continued inquiry. At the extension center, students may select a research question on neuroanatomy, cognition, psychology, positive psychology, or other related fields. You can write these questions by pulling from the content in this book or you can author questions together as a class. Once students have selected a question, they can use their classroom resources, including technology, the media center, and expert guests, to investigate the topic. When a student feels they have a good grasp on their question, they can present their results to the class through a PowerPoint, lecture, blog post, or other presentation. This process helps students nurture their skills as independent investigators.

- **Guest experts:** Invite guest experts to class to share about their work or research and to answer student questions. Neuroscientists, psychologists, biomedical scientists, and neurologists could all add important information to the class's study of the brain. These professionals can also expose students to careers they may not have known about. While organizing guest presentations, remember that representation matters. Seek out women scientists, professionals of color, professionals with disabilities, and experts whose lived experiences are both similar and dissimilar to those of your students. Part of democratizing neuroscience is showing young people that science is for everyone.

Chapter 2

Interrogative Inquiry

ESSENTIAL QUESTION

- How can you use questions as a tool for inquiry?

BIG IDEAS IN SCIENCE

- Cause and Effect
- Cultivating Curiosity

Questions: A Key to Classroom Engagement

What is 5 times 7?

Likely, your first semiautonomous thought was: 35.

If this question caught your attention long enough for you to register it (and this is a big "if" in the classroom), then your brain likely retrieved the answer. You did so regardless of whether you were already thinking about multiplication facts. In fact, I doubt you were thinking about multiplication facts. Maybe you are reading this chapter in the teacher's lounge while running copies for your upcoming science lesson, or while cooking pasta for dinner. Regardless, when presented with a question, your brain paused what it was previously paying attention to in order to answer it. Teachers can make this same intentioned pause happen for students, particularly with more interesting questions than basic multiplication facts.

Once you answered 5 × 7, your second thought was likely "Why?" or "What's the point?" This is an important question. It's also a more interesting question. What makes this question of relevance more interesting than my question of multiplication? Why do both of these questions matter in the classroom, and what do either of them have to do with neuroscience?

Teachers know that questions spark thinking. However, not all questions illicit the same depth or complexity of thinking. A thoughtful or surprising question can foster classroom dialogue and engagement in ways that statements often cannot. Questions give brains space to wonder and make connections. Facts may give brains something to remember, or they may become noise that brains forget. Brain-based classrooms don't leave this to chance. Instead, they constantly facilitate neurological connections across memory, information, and curiosity through the generative power of questions and the magic of higher order thinking questions.

KEY CONCEPT

Bloom's taxonomy: A hierarchical system to classify learning tasks. The original taxonomy was named for Benjamin Bloom (1956), who chaired the committee. In 2001, Anderson and Krathwohl released a revised taxonomy that also accounted for metacognitive processes/ learning objectives. The revised taxonomy includes the following thinking tasks in order of complexity: remember, understand, apply, analyze, evaluate, create.

In his work on brain-based learning, David Sousa (2017) celebrated the "lessening of the [Bloom's] hierarchy" (p. 293) proposed by the 2001 revision. As researchers have learned about cognitive processing, they have come to understand that different cerebral regions are involved in different kinds of thinking tasks. That is, Bloom's taxonomy represents less of a linear approach to becoming a higher order critical thinker and more of a constellation of different types of thinking tasks. This is also why a student may be able to engage with complex tasks that ask them to synthesize or create in a lesson even if they didn't remember all of the facts beforehand. In fact, this is seen in gifted programs all of the time.

Using questions in the classroom isn't new. However, thinking about them through the lens of neuroscience might be. Neuroscientists have made important discoveries about how a concept or idea can capture people's attention. The shorthand version is that people pay attention to the things that are interesting to them (Medina, 2014). This is, of course, complicated in classrooms where many different things may be interesting to different learners. A compelling question can help bridge the attention preferences between diverse learners. In order for a topic to be compelling, students need enough background knowledge to enter the discussion. This is what I like to call "a connecting spark."

Generally, the more complicated the question, the more higher order thinking processes, connections, and retrievals are needed to answer it. Teaching students about different kinds of questions (and different kinds of thinking tasks) can help them think more critically about the processes needed to answer these questions. In the classroom, we often talk about levels of questions (e.g., this is a Level 1 question, etc.). Although different educators have adapted the idea of leveled questions to fit the varying needs of their classrooms, the basic premise is the same: Strive for a range of complexity in the questions both asked and answered. Figure 4 is an anchor chart you can use as you plan lessons to help students write more complex questions.

Why Questions Are Essential

An essential question (EQ) serves as an anchor to a lesson or unit. EQs are higher level thinking questions that invite multiple perspectives. These questions have divergent right answers and layered possibilities.

FIGURE 4
Levels of Questions Anchor Chart

	Level of Question	Definition	Examples	Complexity
Interacting With Information Recalling and using information that is known and understood.	1. Recall Questions	Questions that can be answered with facts. These questions have one correct answer.	• What is 5 × 7? • Who was the third president of the United States? • What are the four lobes of the brain?	Less Complex
	2. Concept Questions	Questions that require connecting readily available information to make a basic connection or inference.	• What is the main point of the article? • What happens to water when heated above the boiling point? • What evidence did the detective find that helped solve the mystery?	
Extending Information Building new connections and ideas by drawing on concepts outside of the original information.	3. Strategic Questions	Questions that require complex reasoning to build on existing information. These questions may have multiple appropriate answers.	• What do you think might happen if we heated butter instead of water? • What would happen if we didn't have speeding laws? • Which of the four lobes is most important, and why?	
	4. Stretch Questions	Questions that ask students to apply concepts from one area to another. These questions have many possibilities and possible answers.	• Is history more shaped by great people or great forces? • What is the most important question for neuroscientists to explore? • How can we use multiplication to create art?	More Complex

An essential question is a critical component of your lesson's anticipatory set that guides the course of study and tethers assessment strategies. The intentional use of essential questions can "support students with opportunities for differentiated learning experiences by examining essential understanding and developing thinking and project-based skills that are the foundation for advanced learning" (MacFarlane, 2018, p. 115). Essential questions invite curiosity and dialogue about a subject. Great essential questions often lead to more questions. In fact, the generative power of questions is part of why questions are the key to inquiry. See Figure 5 for a helpful checklist for writing essential questions.

Leveraging Deeper Levels of Inquiry

Wilson and Smetana (2009) pointed to three widely used classroom practices that facilitate questioning as a metacognitive practice: think-alouds, question-answer-relationships, and self-questioning (p. 20). Teachers can use questions in their classrooms to leverage deeper levels of inquiry. A good starting place is with the questions students pose themselves. Authorship and ownership go together. Students are more invested and engaged in answering the questions they care about. Creating space for and inviting students to pose questions help center curiosity in the classroom. In an article on curiosity in the classroom, Coxon (2018) remarked on the unfortunate decline in academic curiosity that occurs between elementary and secondary school. He argued that young children are naturally curious. I suspect this has less to do with neurology and more to do with the fact that curiosity is actively encouraged and positively reinforced in elementary, especially early-elementary, classrooms. Although this seems like great news for elementary teachers, it also means they have a tremendous responsibility to honor the curiosity of student scholars so that they continue asking questioning and demonstrating curiosity as they move into middle and high school.

A Note About Perceptiveness

How do people sometimes sense when something is right or wrong? What happens when an idea just strikes a person? Perception or intuition refers to unconscious cognitive processes. Colloquially, this is sometimes called "thinking from your gut." It's a sense-making mechanism that is difficult to describe and ubiquitous to the human condition. Neurologically speaking, perception happens in the basal ganglia (Koch, 2015).

> **FIGURE 5**
> A Checklist for Writing Essential Questions
>
> ❏ The question is open-ended.
>
> ❏ The question requires higher order thinking to answer.
>
> ❏ The question is composed of clear and concise language.
>
> ❏ The question invites many possible "right" answers. (Two students can have very different, yet equally compelling and "correct," responses to the question.)
>
> ❏ Learners will be able to refine their ideas about this question over time.
>
> ❏ Answering this essential question requires learners to engage with the key concepts and terms from the unit.
>
> ❏ There are multiple creative ways that students might approach this question.
>
> ❏ The question is a Level 4 question.

NEUROANATOMICAL TIDBIT

Basal ganglia: A group of subcortical nuclei responsible for motor control, motor learning, executive functions and behaviors, and emotions. fMRI studies show that basal ganglia play an important role in intuition (Lanciego et al., 2012).

Perceptiveness is often cited as a characteristic of gifted youth and adults; it translates to an ability to understand several layers of a situation simultaneously, often leading to astute insights and a deep need for truth (Lovecky, 2011). Some neuroscience studies have shown that individuals have great perspective skills in their expert areas. For example, highly accomplished chess players are able to quickly perceive the board, pieces, potential future moves, and strategies almost subconsciously. Practice and experience certainly play a critical role in the ability to perceive situations. In fact, at a biological level, perception is the rapid coding of previous experience that informs current insights or behaviors. Students' interests and expertise areas (which are not always the same) shed important light on the questions that matter most to them and the projects they want to explore.

How teachers encourage students to become independent investigators may be among the most important tools in cultivating curiosity. Student-authored questions can be the impetus for powerful personal inquiry projects. As Coxon (2018) wrote,

> Teachers asking higher order questions in class is important, but it is when students ask those kinds of questions . . . that . . . curiosity is deepened. . . . When students are able to focus their curiosity on an area of interest, they begin to think and work like scientists. (p. 284)

Further, student begin to think like social scientists, mathematicians, engineers, artists, and philosophers.

Encourage your students to question, even if it derails your best-laid lesson plans for a few hours. Students should excitedly chase down answers, wonder, and be "cognitively active" in the process of thinking and learning (Stanger-Hall, 2012). This chapter offers activities to get kids questioning and keep them curious. These activities are merely a starting place or springboard. They come alive in different ways based on the questions and connections your students and classroom environments bring to them.

KEY TERMS FOR EDUCATORS

- **Essential question (EQ):** An interrogative anchor to a lesson or unit. EQs are higher level thinking questions about essential themes in the unit of study.
- **Curiosity:** Inquisitive thinking that includes exploration, investigation, learning, and wonder.
- **Interrogative inquiry:** Using questions to understand or explore something.

Classroom Application

Unit Overview

This unit highlights the importance of questioning as a tool for inquiry. First, students brainstorm questions in their individualized interest areas. Drafting question lists serve two important metacognitive purposes: (1) Students practice questioning as a strategy for exploring thoughts, and (2) teachers gain information about students' curiosities. This information allows for meaningful extension and connection activities. Next, students look at two examples of how questioning can drive wisdom and creation. They read and respond to a text on Socrates and the Socratic Method, and on Georgia O'Keeffe and American Modernism. All problem solvers use questions. Therefore, teaching students about the power of questions can become a cross-curricular tether in your study of famous people in science, mathematics, music, literature, the arts, and social studies. Encouraging students to consider what questions drove the thought processes of leaders, philosophers, artists, engineers, and politicians is an engaging framework for inquiry-based dialogues. Students then author their own question map and review essential terms and ideas.

Time Suggestions

Class 1 (20 minutes)	Class 2 (30 minutes)	Class 3 (30 minutes)	Class 4 (30 minutes)	Extension (variable)
• Handout 2.1: The Place Where Curiosity Begins • Essential Question and Learning Objectives	• Handout 2.2: The 30-Question Challenge	• Handout 2.3: A Brief Introduction to the Socratic Method • Handout 2.4: Georgia O'Keeffe and Questions in Art	• Handout 2.5: Make it Stick!: Interrogative Inquiry	• Extending and Transferring the Concept

STUDENT ACTIVITIES
Interrogative Inquiry

Essential Question

- How can you use questions as a tool for inquiry?

Learning Objectives

By the end of this unit, I will . . .
- practice a metacognitive strategy called interrogative inquiry,
- brainstorm questions to investigate,
- learn about Socrates and the Socratic Method,
- learn about Georgia O'Keeffe and American Modernism, and
- apply interrogative inquiry by creating a question map.

Interrogative Inquiry

HANDOUT 2.1
The Place Where Curiosity Begins

Curiosity often begins with an interesting question to jumpstart your thinking. Questions give your imagination a chance to consider why things are the way they are, how things work, how things came to be, and how things might be different.

An interesting question demands your brain's attention. Once a compelling question is posed, you start thinking about it almost immediately. Let's try it:

> Pretend you are an astronaut who has just landed on the moon. As you tumble out of the spaceship, still uncertain about the gravity of this rocky surface, what is the first thing you do?

Where did your brain go? A moment ago you were reading this text. Then, all of a sudden you were considering what you would do in your first moon landing. That is the power of a question.

Young people like you are often better than adults at asking interesting questions. Questions are the force that leads to new inventions, movements, discoveries, creative projects, and possibilities.

Questions can be silly or serious, happy or sad. You might ask questions about the things you have experienced or the things you have only dreamt about.

What questions are rattling around in your brain?

1. _____

   _____

2. _____

   _____

3. _____

   _____

4. _____

   _____

5. _____

   _____

Interrogative Inquiry

HANDOUT 2.2

The 30-Question Challenge

Write 10 questions beginning with *why* . . .

Example: Why does Earth have only one moon?

1. Why _____

   _____?

2. Why _____

   _____?

3. Why _____

   _____?

4. Why _____

   _____?

5. Why _____

   _____?

6. Why _____

   _____?

7. Why _____

   _____?

8. Why _____

   _____?

9. Why _____

   _____?

10. Why _____

   _____?

Often the first questions very young children ask are "why" questions. "Why" questions ask for an explanation. They point to the things the questioners want to know more about.

Interrogative Inquiry

Name: _____ Date: _____

Write 10 questions beginning with *how* . . .

Example: How do airplanes fly?

1. How _____
   _____?

2. How _____
   _____?

3. How _____
   _____?

4. How _____
   _____?

5. How _____
   _____?

6. How _____
   _____?

7. How _____
   _____?

8. How _____
   _____?

9. How _____
   _____?

10. How _____
   _____?

"How" questions are used to understand processes and relationships. "How" questions are especially important to engineers and problem solvers.

Interrogative Inquiry

HANDOUT 2.2, *continued*

Write 10 questions beginning with *what if* . . .

Example: What if people didn't feel sadness?

1. What if_____
   _____?

2. What if_____
   _____?

3. What if_____
   _____?

4. What if_____
   _____?

5. What if_____
   _____?

6. What if_____
   _____?

7. What if_____
   _____?

8. What if_____
   _____?

9. What if_____
   _____?

10. What if_____
    _____?

"What if" questions are used to spark imagination. These questions allow you to think about if things were different. These are the questions of dreamers.

Interrogative Inquiry

Analyzing Your 30 Questions

1. Circle your most interesting questions.
2. Put a star next to the question you want to start exploring first.
3. What patterns do you notice in your questions? Are there topics you seem especially interested in? If so, what are they?

_____

_____

_____

_____

_____

Often one question leads to another question, and then another, and so on. Once we start wondering why something is the way it is or imagining new possibilities, we find there is a lot more we want to learn. Questioning is a powerful practice in inquiry. Asking interesting questions is how inventions are made, how new solutions are found, and how we make progress as people.

Interrogative Inquiry

HANDOUT 2.3

A Brief Introduction to the Socratic Method

SOCRATES, a Greek philosopher, lived 2,500 years ago in a city called Athens. Although he had many interests, including sculpture and poetry, Socrates is most remembered for his contributions to **philosophy**, or the study of knowledge and reality. Philosophers ask questions about truth, science, logic, and learning.

During Socrates's lifetime, most people who were interested in understanding the world, looked to science for answers. Socrates thought people should also look to human behavior for answers. He believed people could learn a lot by paying attention to the ways they treat one another. Socrates was interested in exploring right and wrong. He was interested in why some people were happier than others and also in how to encourage people to make a positive difference in the world.

Can you guess how Socrates gathered his information? He used questions or an **interrogative** approach. Socrates both asked and listened to interesting questions. He was interested in wisdom and believed that if people paid attention they could find it everywhere. In fact, he often found that people who were not considered experts asked some of the best questions.

Socrates developed a new method for **inquiry**. Inquiry is a way to gather information. As you have probably guessed, his method encouraged lots of questions. In the **Socratic Method**, people work together using questions and logic in an attempt to discover the truth.

Interrogative Inquiry

Name: _____ Date: _____

Comprehension and Reflection Questions

1. Who was Socrates? _____
   _____
   _____

2. What kinds of questions was Socrates interested in?_____
   _____
   _____

3. What kinds of questions are you interested in? _____
   _____
   _____

4. Socrates believed that people who were not considered experts often asked the most interesting questions. Why do you think that is?
   _____
   _____
   _____

5. What is inquiry? How might a neuroscientist use inquiry in their work?
   _____
   _____
   _____

6. How can you use questions to better understand what you are learning?
   _____
   _____
   _____

7. Would you consider yourself a philosopher? Why or why not? Do you think Socrates would think you were a philosopher?
   _____
   _____
   _____

Interrogative Inquiry

HANDOUT 2.4

Georgia O'Keeffe and Questions in Art

"Nobody sees a flower—really—it is so small it takes time—we haven't time—and to see takes time, like to have a friend takes time."
—Georgia O'Keeffe

GEORGIA O'KEEFFE was a famous American artist who lived from 1887 to 1986. Artists ask questions about **perspective**, or the way a person sees something. One of the questions O'Keeffe asked was, "What if we looked at flowers differently?" This question led to her most famous paintings, which are giant close-ups of flowers. O'Keeffe said that by painting her flowers big, she forced people to stop and pay attention. She believed people don't pay enough attention.

Who is art for? What topics should artists explore? How does art represent life? These were guiding questions that Georgia O'Keeffe both asked and answered in her work. O'Keeffe believed that art was for everyone. She worked at a time when women artists were not given much attention. Her work both demanded and received attention, inspiring all and particularly encouraging girls and women to pursue art.

O'Keeffe believed that artists could be everyday people and should explore everyday scenes. She also thought that art could be used to explain and to discover. These ideas about art began a movement called **American Modernism**.

In her 80s, Georgia O'Keeffe went blind, so she asked another question: "How can I keep making art?" She found her answer through sculpture, which she continued making until she passed away at almost 100 years old.

Questions drive creation. What questions will you answer in your own creative work?

Interrogative Inquiry

HANDOUT 2.4, *continued*

Comprehension and Reflection Questions

1. Who was Georgia O'Keeffe? _____

   _____

   _____

2. What are some of the questions she asked through art? _____

   _____

   _____

3. How did O'Keeffe make people pay attention? _____

   _____

   _____

4. O'Keeffe said, "Nobody sees a flower—really—it is so small it takes time—we haven't time—and to see takes time, like to have a friend takes time." What do you think she meant when she said having a friend takes time?

   _____

   _____

   _____

5. How can people use art to help them learn? _____

   _____

   _____

6. How can people use art to share their ideas? _____

   _____

   _____

7. Do you consider yourself an artist? Why or why not? _____

   _____

   _____

Interrogative Inquiry

HANDOUT 2.5

Make It Stick!: Interrogative Inquiry

In this unit, we learned that questions are cognitively powerful and **generative** (meaning one question leads to another, and then another, and so on). Questioning leads to many connections in the brain.

Challenge: Question Map

Choose one interesting question that you want to explore and create a question map around it. You might choose the question you starred in the 30-Question Challenge, or you might have another question you are ready to chase down.

> ### KEY TERMS
>
> **Interrogative inquiry:** Using questions to gather more information.
>
> **Socrates:** A Greek philosopher who lived from 470–399 BC. He is credited with the Socratic Method, which uses questions in order to help people get closer to understanding truth.
>
> **Philosophy:** The study of knowledge and reality.
>
> **Inquiry:** Investigating or seeking information.
>
> **Socratic Method:** Using questions and working together to discover truth.
>
> **Georgia O'Keeffe:** A famous American artist who started the American Modernism movement.
>
> **Perspective:** The way you see something.

Guidelines

- Write your question on the center of the page.
- Draw spikes coming off of your question.
- At the end of each spike, write related questions. If possible, group these new questions together by category.
- Once you have a full page of questions, add information around the questions, such as connections, ideas, and resources.
- At the top of the page, write what sparked your question (e.g., a story, an article, an experience).
- At the bottom of the page, write what you are going to do next with all of these thoughts (e.g., a research or art project).

Interrogative Inquiry

Extending and Transferring the Concept

The following are several ideas to extend and transfer interrogative inquiry beyond the activities in this chapter. Keep building on the ways that questions capture students' attention and continue adding ideas to cultivate a classroom culture marked by curiosity and wonder.

Handout 2.1: The Place Where Curiosity Begins

- **Think-pair-share:** Why are young people often better than adults at asking interesting questions?
- **Prediction board:** At the beginning of this unit, give each student a sticky note and ask them to write what they think interrogative inquiry is. At the end of the unit, ask students to revise their answers.

Handout 2.2: The 30-Question Challenge

- **Independent research:** Invite students to research the question they starred and present their answers to the class.
- **Teach leveled questions:** Ask students to analyze their questions to determine what levels of questions they have written.
  - Do certain question words tend to lead to certain kinds of questions?
  - Can students edit their questions to make them more complex?

- **Class discussion:** Which questions are the most interesting to generate?
- **Make connections:** Have students compare and contrast their question lists in groups of four. What patterns do they notice?
- **Work with a partner:** Have students work in pairs to develop 10 more "how" questions. After pairs share their lists, discuss how this process is different when students work together.
- **Make a film:** Working as a class, film a short documentary on this prompt: *Why do questions matter?* Try to include as many concepts from this unit as possible.

Handout 2.3: A Brief Introduction to the Socratic Method

- **Hold a Socratic Seminar:** Use your students' "what if" questions as discussion prompts in this Socratic Seminar.
- **Research more about Socrates:** Ask students to explore more about Socrates's life, death, and contributions to philosophy. Students should present their findings and answer the question: *What can Socrates teach us about metacognition?*
- **Create a philosophy timeline:** Ask students to create a timeline illustrating the teaching-learning relationships of Socrates, Plato, Aristotle, and Alexander the Great. Assign students to expert groups to research one of these thinkers. Groups can then present to the class and add their findings to the class timeline.

Handout 2.4: Georgia O'Keeffe and Questions in Art

- **Create a giant painting:** Share the following prompt: *O'Keeffe made people pay attention by painting small things big. What is something you think people should pay more attention to? Create a giant painting around this idea.*
- **Explore the connection between art and thinking:** Invite guest artists and other professionals to speak to your class on how they can use drawing and visuals to think through problems.
- **Take a walking field trip:** The American Modernism movement stressed that art was for everyone and that everyday scenes and objects could inspire art. Take a walking field trip through your community, looking for inspiration in everyday scenes. Ask students: *What can we learn when we view our community through the lens of an artist?*

Additional Extensions

- **Interrogative audit with students:** Teachers often do an excellent job of both using questions to prompt inquiry and encouraging a culture of curiosity by making space for student questions. Still, it never hurts to do an interrogative audit of your classroom by tracking the number of questions you pose in your lessons and the number of questions students offer in a class day. It can be difficult to track these data on your own, so I recommend getting your students involved. If you have a classroom aide or paraprofessional, they may be able to help as well. Ask your students to tally up the number of questions they hear. Having just completed these activities, students will know how important questions are to learning and may be excited to engage in this research. The volume of questions may also be a bit higher following an inquiry lesson, and that is okay!

You and your students can also create interrogative categories to track. Possible categories include: open versus closed questions, questions by teacher versus questions by students, questions that stay within the lesson versus questions that lead to the exploration of a new concept, etc. Use the data to look for patterns. Do you pose questions at the beginning of the lesson but then less often throughout the day? Are certain groups asking more questions than others? Are you hearing mostly open questions or closed questions? The interrogative audit is not a critique on your classroom practice but an iterative tool that you and your students can use together to make meaningful changes.

KEY CONCEPT

Interrogative audit: A classwide data project aimed at assessing the volume of questions posed during a lesson (by teachers and students) to analyze the types and patterns of questions being offered in class.

- **Question journal:** Encourage students to keep their own question journals. Once they get in the habit, gifted students will likely find they have many questions about all facets of the universe. To jumpstart the practice, challenge students to write 10–30 questions a day. Students can use their question journal as inspiration for personal research and inquiry projects by seeking answers to a question from their list. For more ideas about using question journals, check out Gelb's (2004) *How to Think Like Leonardo da Vinci: Seven Steps to Genius Every Day*.
- **Famous thinkers:** When studying famous thinkers, ask students: *What question or questions do you think they were most interested in answering?* After learning, research, and exploration, return to this idea and ask how those thinkers answered their essential question(s). This practice teaches students that innovation is born not through already knowing an answer, but through chasing a question.

- **Content questions:** When introducing a new concept or content, ask students: *What question(s) is this field most interested in exploring?* You can use these questions in applied lessons to help students think like an engineer, mathematician, historian, etc.
- **Question box:** Keep a box of big questions in your classroom. Use one of these questions as a discussion topic when you have 10 minutes at the end of class. Students can also explore these questions on their own when they have independent work time. Invite all students to contribute big questions to the question box. Monitor the question box for both curiosity patterns and school appropriateness.
- **What questions do you have?:** Teachers often ask students what they notice in a new text, picture, or experience. This honors the different perspectives young people bring to lessons. Try also asking students: *What questions do you have about this?* See how the answers shift. This framing sends the message that questioning is part of processing. Remind gifted students that they don't have to know everything about a subject in order to bring important and interesting perspectives to the class community.

Chapter 3

Maximizing Metacognitive Moments

ESSENTIAL QUESTION

- How are metacognition and learning connected?

BIG IDEAS IN SCIENCE

- Cause and Effect
- Patterns

BRAIN-BASED Learning With Gifted Students

Why Metacognitive Moments Matter

Metacognition comes from the root words *cognition* and *meta*. Cognition is the process of thinking and knowing; it has to do with how people take in information and stimuli and transform them into thoughts, questions, and knowledge. This process requires complex connections involving emotions, senses, reasoning, problem solving, attention, and memory. *Meta* means "above" or "about a thing itself." This is why teachers often tell students that metacognition means "thinking about thinking." Although this definition is a fine starting place, it oversimplifies the positive feedback loop caused by metacognitive practices (Fadel et al., 2015). For this reason, I like to tell students that metacognition is *the way thinking about thinking leads to new thinking, often about thinking.*

KEY CONCEPT

Metacognition: A critical understanding of (1) one's own thinking and learning, and (2) one's identity as a thinker and learner (Chick, 2019); the way thinking about thinking creates a positive feedback loop that leads to greater cognitive awareness.

The Neuroscience of Metacognition

Metacognition was first defined by John H. Flavell, an American developmental psychologist, in 1979. Throughout the 1980s, research about metacognition focused primarily on studies with young children. This research later expanded to adolescents and adults. The benefits of metacognition include an ability to learn more deeply and assign meaning to content (Sousa, 2017) and an ability to transfer learning, thinking processes, and problem-solving models to new contexts (Chick, 2019).

In order for the learning process to begin, the brain must be in conversation with new information. In cognitive terms this is called *initial rehearsal* (Sousa, 2017). *Secondary rehearsal* occurs as learners continue to review information, elaborate on it, and make connections. The frontal lobe is involved in all of these processes, and with enough meaningful rehearsal, the information is able to move from the working memory to long-term memory. Rehearsal and metacognition go hand-in-hand. Teachers can support the learning and rehearsal process by giving students key questions to help them connect new information with previously learned information. Teachers can also encourage students to ask questions about the material (see Chapter 2) so that they deepen their conversation and connections with class material and interact with the content more fully.

56

KEY CONCEPT

Rehearsal: The reprocessing of information. Rehearsal is critical in moving information from working memory to long-term memory (Sousa, 2017).

Even after a new concept is "learned," metacognition continues to be important in the learning process. This is because concepts don't exist in isolation. Instead, what a student learns in one context or class relates to concepts encountered in other places. Metacognition assists with this transfer. When a student who is well-versed in metacognition arrives at a challenging math problem, difficult text, or complicated social interaction, they have the tools to ask themselves why this situation is challenging them and what they can do to process or mediate the challenge. Metacognition can quiet negative self-talk and promote self-regulation (Jacobson, 2019).

Neuroscientists and researchers at the University College London recently reported that subjects with stronger metacognition skills and tendencies had more gray matter in the anterior (frontal) prefrontal cortex (Wilson & Conyers, 2014).

NEUROANATOMICAL TIDBIT

Gray matter is a major structure of the central nervous system. It consists primarily of neuronal cell bodies, called *soma*, which contain the neuron's nucleus. Gray matter is found throughout the cerebellum, cerebrum, brain stem, and spinal cord. It is most concentrated in the cerebellum. Although the gray matter in the cerebellum contains more neurons than the rest of the brain combined, the cerebral cortex neurons play a critical role in almost all aspects of cognition.

Late elementary and early middle school students have the most gray matter density in their prefrontal cortex. In the developing human brain, gray matter volume tends to increase until puberty (Gogtay & Thompson, 2010). Gray matter density in the frontal lobe tends to peak around age 11 and then begins to decline. This is yet another reason that late elementary and early middle school is an optimal time to build a foundation for metacognitive practices.

Metacognition and Gifted Learners

In gifted and talented classrooms, teachers work with students who learn differently and who often exhibit asynchronous (or uneven) development. This means that a student may be very advanced in one area (e.g., math reasoning) and still struggling in another (e.g., fine motor). These students may have some cognitive processes more typical of older students (e.g., reading comprehension) and other processes more typical of younger students (e.g., emotional regulation). For twice-exceptional (2e) students, these idiosyncratic differences are even more pronounced.

Unfortunately, gifted students are sometimes left out of the literature or practice of metacognitive programs in schools. Research shows that gifted and talented students tend to exhibit a higher aptitude for metacognition; therefore, the emphasis on these programs and research is on "struggling learners." Gifted educators know that the schism between aptitude and actualization is only mended by intentionality and practice. The research on talent development shows that the consequences of assuming that aptitude will make up for instruction tends to negate aptitude altogether. Therefore, although gifted students may have the capacity for higher order metacognitive processing, if these skills are not nurtured, they may lose them. When the cognitive and affective needs of gifted students are not met,

> they can come to feel there is something wrong with them, and to be ashamed of their talents. Exceptionally gifted children are children at risk, as much as are children whose achievement is below average. It is hoped that by understanding these gifted children's unique cognitive characteristics, their talents can be appreciated and further developed. (Lovecky, 1994, para. 44)

Teaching metacognition helps students understand their unique constellation of thoughts, behaviors, and feelings, and puts them in charge of their own learning and thinking.

Fostering problem solving and positive self-talk is an especially important intervention for gifted students who may struggle with either perfectionism (Schuler, 2002) or underachievement (Reis & McCoach, 2002; Winton, 2013), both of which are cited as important counseling foci for gifted populations. Lovecky (1994) argued that support for the cognitive needs of exceptionally gifted students (>170) are even more lacking in school programs, particularly as acceleration and advancement has become less common. Metacognition can be a powerful framework to help students drive their learning by exploring their own thinking processes, interrogating personal interest quandaries, and solving highly personal problems that matter to them.

Metacognition is included in the NAGC (2019) programming standards. Under the talent development strand, educators working with gifted and talented youth are charged to support young people as they "become more competent in multiple talent areas and across dimensions of learning." They can do this through modeling and teaching metacognitive practices to support "self-assessment, goal setting, and monitoring of learning." Recent research in neuroscience has shown how powerful it is to teach students about thinking, cognition, and problem-solving models. Within dense curricula, making intentional space for students to think (and learn) about thinking is important. The activities in this chapter offer a strong starting place to introduce young people to metacognition.

Fostering Metacognitive Moments

Classrooms are busy. If teachers are not vigilant, they can miss metacognitive teaching moments. Focusing on maximizing the right moments can alter the way teachers (and students) make meaning in classrooms. Students should actively think about their thinking, learning, and doing processes as frequently as possible. This chapter offers a list of sample questions you can use to infuse metacognition into your daily classroom practices. The activities in this chapter use these questions as a springboard for paying more attention to your *thinking self-talk*. By building reflexive thinking opportunities into curriculum, teachers can help students better explore the depths and dimensions of their own thinking.

KEY TERMS FOR EDUCATORS

- **Asynchronous:** Uneven; not existing at the same time.
- **Gray matter:** A major structure of the central nervous system consisting primarily of neuronal cell bodies, called *soma*, which contain the neuron's nucleus.
- **Metacognitive moment:** An ordinary moment that teaches students about their thinking.

- **Rehearsal:** The reprocessing of information.
- **Soma:** Neuronal cell bodies (see *gray matter*).
- **Thinking self-talk:** The inner monologue a person has about their own thinking.

Classroom Application

Unit Overview

This unit highlights the importance of listening to one's thinking self-talk. Students learn about the concepts of thinking self-talk and metacognition. Students are encouraged to pay attention to the messages they give themselves about their own thinking and look for ways they can be more encouraging or kind to themselves. Each of the three activities following the springboard reading addresses different metacognitive questions.

First, students solve a complicated maze. This activity gives students a low-stakes challenge to observe how they track their progress on a task and respond when they are not on track. After completing the provided maze, students are challenged to design their own maze. This task requires complex problem solving and also includes the opportunity to teach others about this concept.

Next, students work on making divergent and creative connections. Students are shown four artifacts that do not have obvious similarities. They are asked to respond to these artifacts individually and in different sets. This task asks them to seek similarities, make connections, and defend their thinking.

The last practice activity in this unit is to venture a creative risk on common classroom assignments. Students are given three standard class assignments and asked how they could offer new solutions and ideas to these assignments. Although students may certainly also complete the assignments, their primary task is to think through how they could take a creative or novel approach to the assignment. Could they use different materials? Could they present the information in a new way? Could they use unexpected examples? This challenge gives students practice transferring this brain-based concept to other content.

In the summative project, students are asked to design a comic strip featuring Metis, Greek goddess of wisdom, as she teaches another character about the importance of metacognition. Also included are "make it stick" materials and thought questions that students may use as they work on their comic strips and continue to transfer these skills.

Time Suggestions

Class 1 *(20 minutes)*	Class 2 *(30 minutes)*	Class 3 *(20 minutes)*	Class 4 *(30 minutes)*	Extension *(variable)*
▪ Handout 3.1: Thinking About Thinking Leads to New Thinking ▪ Essential Question and Learning Objectives	▪ Handout 3.2: Am I on Track? ▪ Handout 3.3: Can I Make a Connection?	▪ Handout 3.4: Can I Take a Creative Risk?	▪ Handout 3.5: Make It Stick!: Maximizing Meta-cognitive Moments	▪ Extending and Transferring the Concept

STUDENT ACTIVITIES

Maximizing Metacognitive Moments

Essential Question

■ How are metacognition and learning connected?

Learning Objectives

By the end of this unit, I will be able to . . .
■ define metacognition,
■ practice answering metacognitive questions,
■ develop strategies to maximize metacognitive moments, and
■ explain why metacognition matters in learning.

Name: _____ Date: _____

Thinking About Thinking Leads to New Thinking

How much do you know about yourself as a thinker? One clue is to pay attention to your self-talk. **Self-talk** is the voice inside your head. It is the way you talk to yourself as you go about life.

What does your self-talk sound like when you are working out a challenging problem? Do you encourage yourself? If you get stuck, do you think about another solution to try? Or do you get frustrated, feel angry, and give up? Does it depend on the problem? What kinds of challenges do you most enjoy solving?

These are all metacognitive questions. **Metacognition** is the way that thinking about your thinking leads to new thinking, often about . . . thinking. Metacognition matters. It can help you be a more effective problem solver, scholar, and citizen. And like most things, metacognition is something you can improve with practice.

One way to become more proficient at metacognition is to listen to your thinking self-talk and try to make it more positive and productive. Encourage yourself, just as you would encourage a younger sibling or a friend. You can take charge of your self-talk, even when solving complex problems or dealing with frustrating situations. In fact, noticing that something is frustrating and committing to think through it can be a metacognitive moment.

Metacognitive moments are ordinary moments when you learn something new about your own thinking.

HANDOUT 3.1, *continued*

Comprehension and Reflection Questions

1. What does your thinking self-talk sound like? _____

_____

_____

_____

2. When are you most encouraging to yourself? _____

_____

_____

_____

3. When could you be kinder to yourself? _____

_____

_____

_____

4. What types of problems (or challenges) do you enjoy working on? _____

_____

_____

_____

5. Describe a time when you learned something new about who you are as a thinker.

_____

_____

_____

_____

Maximizing Metacognitive Moments

HANDOUT 3.2
Am I on Track?

There are many powerful metacognitive questions you can use while working on a project or problem. A good one to start with is: *Am I on track?* It is helpful to notice when things are going well. It is just as helpful, or maybe even more so, to notice when things are not going well. Noticing whether or not you are on track is a metacognitive moment.

Challenge

Complete the following maze starting at the bottom left. Please note, this maze is *not* a test of your problem-solving skills as much as it is an opportunity to practice persistence (and possibly some visual processing). **Persistence** means continuing to work even when things aren't going well. In this task, you will likely run into some dead ends. As you do, pay attention to your thinking self-talk. Are you being kind to yourself? Are you persisting? Are you trying to look ahead to see if your choices are keeping you on track?

Follow-Up Challenge

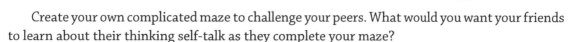

Create your own complicated maze to challenge your peers. What would you want your friends to learn about their thinking self-talk as they complete your maze?

Brain-Based Learning With Gifted Students © Prufrock Press Inc.

Maximizing Metacognitive Moments

Name: _____ Date: _____

Can I Make a Connection?

Connecting ideas, experiences, and information strengthens the neural pathways in your brain. Does something you are reading remind you of something else you have read or experienced personally? Does the problem or challenge you are working on remind you of another problem you have worked through? Can you find a similar theme between two or more things that seemed unrelated? Making these connections is a metacognitive practice.

Challenge: Connections

Directions: Look at the four cells below and answer the connection questions.

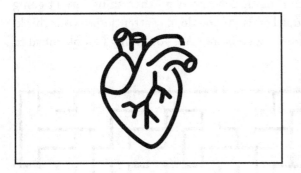

If you're always trying to be normal you will never know how amazing you can be.

—*Maya Angelou*

$2^3 = 2 \times 2 \times 2$

1. Which cell(s) do you find the most interesting, and why? _____

_____

_____

_____

_____

HANDOUT 3.3, *continued*

2. Which cell is the most uniquely human? Defend your answer. _____

_____

_____

_____

_____

3. Choose two (or more) of the cells. What is something they have in common?

_____

_____

_____

_____

_____

4. Choose two (or more) of the cells. Make a new connection. _____

_____

_____

_____

_____

5. Now look at all four cells together. What themes do they have in common? If someone were to use all of these to teach a lesson or tell a story, what would it be about?

_____

_____

_____

_____

_____

HANDOUT 3.4

Can I Take a Creative Risk?

Creativity is the magic that makes new ideas possible. However, not all creative ideas work, especially the first time. Sometimes they fail or flop. Creative risks are risks; this means the outcome is unknown. The good news is that sometimes when a creative idea flops, you can learn even more than had it succeeded.

Every day you have the opportunity to practice creativity. Can you approach a project or assignment in a way that no one else has tried? Imagining new and creative ideas is a powerful metacognitive practice.

Challenge

Directions: Brainstorm ideas for taking creative risks on the following three assignments. You might think about using different materials, presenting the information in a way no else has considered, testing an idea that requires bravery, or using unexpected examples.

- **Assignment 1:** Write a multiplication story problem.
- **Assignment 2:** Create a self-portrait.
- **Assignment 3:** Conduct an experiment to test this law in physics: *An object will remain at rest or in constant state of motion unless acted on by an external force.*

Maximizing Metacognitive Moments

HANDOUT 3.5

Make It Stick!: Maximizing Metacognitive Moments

Challenge: Metacognitive Metis Comic Strip

In Greek mythology, Metis was the goddess of wisdom and deep thought. As such, she surely practiced metacognition. For this challenge, create a comic strip in which Metis teaches another character about the importance of metacognition. Make sure her lesson includes specific ways to practice metacognition. You may want to review the metacognitive questions below. You may also want to do some additional research on Metis. Naturally, you will want to look for opportunities to take creative risks.

KEY TERMS

Self-talk: The voice inside your head; the way you talk to yourself as you go about life.

Metacognition: The way thinking about your thinking leads to new thinking, often about thinking.

Metacognitive moments: Ordinary moments when you learn something new about your thinking.

Metis: The Greek goddess of wisdom and deep thought.

Neural pathways: The connections that make synapses to transfer information from one location in the brain to another.

Creativity: Using your imagination to make or do something original and unique.

Persistence: Continuing to work even when things aren't going well.

Metacognitive Questions

⚓ Am I on the right track?

⚓ How do I know if I am on track or not?

⚓ How can I connect this to something else I have learned?

⚓ How can I connect this to my life?

⚓ What will I do if I get stuck?

⚓ Who can I go to with questions about this?

⚓ What am I most proud of accomplishing with this project?

⚓ If I could try again, what would I do differently?

⚓ What does this remind me of?

⚓ Does that answer make sense?

⚓ Where can I take a creative risk?

⚓ How could I convince someone else that my idea is correct?

⚓ How can I take what I learned here and transfer it to another context?

Extending and Transferring the Concept

My hope is that maximizing metacognitive moments becomes an ongoing focus in your classroom practice. The following ideas extend the learning activities in this chapter. Seek out moments to make thinking visible in your classroom. Encourage students to track what they are learning about themselves as thinkers and also to cultivate positive thinking self-talk.

Handout 3.1: Thinking About Thinking Leads to New Thinking

- **Metacognitive memes:** Challenge students to create a meme-like drawing plus text to explain what metacognition is.
- **Thinking self-talk conferences:** This text may lead to important interpersonal discoveries. Take the time to meet with students one-on-one to listen to their reflections on the first thought question.

Handout 3.2: Am I on Track?

- **Socratic Seminar:** It is easy for students to get caught up in solving the maze as quickly as possible and miss the purpose of this activity, which is to shed light on their thinking self-talk. In a Socratic Seminar, challenge students to make connections between solving the maze and other areas of their life or school day. What might the maze represent?
- **Teach others:** As students work on the follow-up challenge either individually or in groups, they will likely realize that making a tricky maze involves creating pathways that seem like they will work but actually lead to dead ends. Encourage students to draw connections between the mazes they make, the mazes they are trying to solve, and their lives. Give students the opportunity to share their completed mazes with other students and teach them about thinking self-talk, metacognition, and responding to challenges.
- **Change the scale:** Challenge students to create a life-size maze or obstacle course that requires persistence to solve.

Handout 3.3: Can I Make a Connection?

- **Connection game:** Working in small groups, place 2–4 items in the center of the table. Challenge students to think of as many different ways to connect the items as possible in 3 minutes. You can have students shout out answers or go around in a circle. Students can suggest new items for subsequent rounds. Think creatively: Although objects work well for this game, you can also choose more abstract things, like the number 7, the letter A, or hope.
- **Writing prompt:** Place 2–4 items (concrete and abstract) at the front of the room. Challenge students to write a story (or poem, song, letter) that includes all of these items.

Handout 3.4: Can I Take a Creative Risk?

- **Test ideas:** In the activity, students propose ways they can take a creative risk on common assignments. To extend this activity, have students carry out their plans and share their final products with their peers.

Handout 3.5: Make It Stick!: *Maximizing Metacognitive Moments*

- **Comic book:** Students can develop a more complex plot and then work together to create a Metacognitive Metis comic book.
- **Metacognitive play:** Students can write and perform a play about metacognition. The play could include other ancient gods and goddesses, or it could be set in current times.

Additional Extensions

Of course, metacognition shouldn't stop with this unit. The following are some ideas to transfer these concepts to other content areas.

- **Brainbook thinker profile:** Most social media sites ask users to create a user profile. Challenge students to create a similar "thinker profile." Instead of Facebook, they might think of this as "Brainbook" (see Figure 6 for a simple template to get your started). Brainbook profiles can include images and text.

FIGURE 6
Brainbook Template

Name: _____

BRAINBOOK

About This Thinker: _____

Scholar Quote: _____ *Highlights:* _____

- **Image ideas:** A project, a problem, or something representative of the kinds of thinking tasks students enjoy (this could also be an image of them engaged in work) and some text saying who they are as a thinker.
- **Text ideas:** A bio or byline about what differentiates them from other thinkers (humor and emoji are welcome).

This project makes a great bulletin board or classwide website. In fact, students can continue building out their Brainbook pages throughout the school year by adding more artifacts and positive comments on their friends' pages. If you are using a physical bulletin board, sticky notes work well for comments. If you invite comments on the Brainbook, establish strong ground rules about kindness ahead of time. This activity pairs well with lessons on social cognition.

- **Metacognitive focus question:** Using the metacognitive questions on Handout 3.5 as a starting place, challenge students to sort questions into three groups: before starting a task/project, during a task/project, and after a task/project. Post these questions in a central location in your classroom and encourage students to add to them throughout the year. Make part of your work or project time selecting a focus question from the board. Students can select individual questions, or you can select class focus questions for the work session.

- **Content-based connection game:** Use the connection game to introduce a new concept, activate prior knowledge, and engage curiosity. For example, if starting a lesson on U.S. civil rights, you might ask students to connect Ruby Bridges, a bus, and 1964. Students can make predictions about the connections, do research, and share what they know. If starting a lesson on exponents, you might ask students if they can draw a connection between multiplication, a parabola graph, and the superscript symbol.

- **Creative risk professional development:** Host a professional development lunch with other classroom teachers in your building on taking creative risks. Feel free to share concepts from this book and the work your students did on the creative risk activities, especially if you also carried out the activities as an extension. This context may help classroom teachers when they see gifted students responding to assignments in new ways. Teachers could even establish a schoolwide focus encouraging all students to consider assignments from multiple perspectives.

Chapter 4

Sparking Connection With Wonder

ESSENTIAL QUESTION

- How can you respond to the world with both wonder and reason?

BIG IDEAS IN SCIENCE

- Patterns
- Cause and Effect
- Interdependence

Unlock Wonder, Unleash Potential

What can psychology and neuroscience teach about wonder or mind-wandering? More than 2,500 years ago, Socrates put it plainly when he said, "All thinking begins with wonder." How can teachers honor and encourage wonder in the classroom, even if wonder looks like daydreaming or mind-wandering? Although scientists have studied the resting brain for several decades (neuromyth alert: the brain doesn't actually rest, but it does help you rest), the *default mode network* (DMN) is a newer concept in neuroscience. Throughout the 1990s, most neuroscientific studies focused on externally based task experiments (Callard et al., 2012). fMRI studies revealed that tasks such as recalling a memory, reflecting, or considering an event in the future are orchestrated and supported by the DMN. That is, the brain's DMN shows greater activity while a person is focused internally rather than externally (Ashwal, 2017).

NEUROANATOMICAL TIDBIT

Default Mode Network (DMN): An interrelated network of brain regions that is active when a person is focused internally. This is sometimes referred to as wakeful rest or self-generated neural activity (Callard et al., 2012). It includes tasks such as reflection, memory recall, and daydreaming.

Mind-wandering is a common, universal condition that occupies close to 50% of daily thinking time (McMillan et al., 2013; Stawarczyk et al., 2012). In the literature, mind-wandering is sometimes referred to as *stimulus-independent and task-unrelated thoughts* (SITUTs; Stawarczyk et al., 2012).

Although teachers of neurodiverse students may be empathetic to various types of mind-wandering, daydreaming is rarely encouraged in class. Rather than mind-wandering, teachers usually encourage focused attention (on teacher-directed materials and objectives). They want students to pay attention to the lesson at hand. They want students to meet and master the essential learning objectives set in the lessons. However, as researchers better understand both the nature (and power) of constructive mind-wandering and the role this kind of internal processing has on reflection, motivation, and creativity, more space should be made for wonder in classrooms.

Positive Constructive Daydreaming

Jerome L. Singer, a psychologist and researcher at Yale University, pioneered work in daydreaming. His research continues to inform understanding of daydreaming, particularly *positive constructive daydreaming* (McMillan et al., 2013). Singer's work to defend daydreaming was revolutionary when he launched his studies in the 1950s. Previously, psychologists and doctors associated mind-wandering and daydreaming with pathology, or something they needed to stop and treat. Singer's studies offered a positive alternative. Singer identified three styles of daydreaming:

- positive constructive daydreaming (playful, wishful, creative),
- guilty-dysphoric daydreaming (obsessive, dark thoughts), and
- poor attentional control (inability to concentrate).

KEY CONCEPT

Positive constructive daydreaming: A term coined by Jerome L. Singer to refer to mind-wandering that is playful, wishful, and creative. This kind of daydreaming can lead to productive behaviors and innovative new ideas. People can even learn to focus their daydreaming so that it is more positively constructive.

Of these three styles of daydreaming, positive constructive daydreaming is the most important to foster in the classroom. Singer and his colleagues (McMillan et al., 2013) associated positive constructive daydreaming with four positive functions:

- Future Planning (supports self-reflection),
- Creativity (assists with problem solving),
- Attentional Cycling (helps persist toward goals), and
- Dishabituation (gives meaningful attentional breaks and opportunities for rehearsal).

The other two styles of daydreaming, guilty-dysphoric daydreaming and poor attentional control, are normal in moderation but can lead to depressive or challenging situations if they become too commonplace or are not processed in real time with supportive networks. Mind-wandering studies have shown that individuals, including young people, can report on their daydreams, giving teachers and families opportunities to process, problem solve, and redirect as needed.

Take Your Idea for a Walk

I often use a strategy called "take your idea for a walk" in my teaching practice. When I notice a student struggling to get started on or continue the lesson at hand, I give them permission to take their idea for a walk. This can look like:

- a physical walk—I've been known to send students to deliver blank envelopes to the office or a partner teacher just to get them up and moving;
- a free write—students can write about whatever their mind is working on; or
- 3 minutes of uninterrupted verbal processing with me.

By honoring that their mind is working and giving them space to wrestle with their divergent ideas, I find that students often return from their idea walks with greater focus on the lesson.

Subregions of the Prefrontal Cortex

The prefrontal cortex (PFC) is essential in helping teachers understand why certain information catches students' attention, how they connect it with previous information, and why they make some of the decisions they make in classrooms.

Making up 10% of the brain, the PFC is the area of the frontal lobe that lies directly behind the forehead. The PFC is important for cognitive processes, particularly executive function, or the ability to plan and persist toward a goal. The PFC supports complex social-emotional and cognitive tasks by receiving information and communicating across the brain to help plan a response.

The PFC is divided into subregions. There is some debate among neuroscientists about the precise division and function of the PFC subregions. For the purposes of this book, this section describes the major divisions along the midline of the body. The PFC is divided into *medial regions* (meaning near the midline of the body) and *lateral regions* (meaning toward the side body).

- **Medial subregions of the PFC:** The *medial prefrontal cortex* (mPFC) and related regions assist with processing and integrating social and affective information (Grossman, 2013). It helps control recent, remote, and emotional memories (Euston et al., 2012). It also is important in generating appropriate motor responses. The *orbitofrontal PFC* (oPFC) assists with decision making, particularly when it comes to assigning value to information and negotiating rewards or consequences.
- **Lateral subregions of the PFC:** The *lateral prefrontal cortex* (lPFC) and related regions are essential in planning and executing complex thinking

tasks, such as speech and logical reasoning (Fuster, 2001). It also supports working memory, persistence toward a goal, and *preparatory set*, or preparing for stressful situations (Payne & Crane-Godreau, 2015).

Although the subregions in the PFC have different roles, neuroscientists stress that the interaction between subregions, or ways these regions work together as an interconnected network, is more important than the individual functions of any of the distinct regions.

The brain develops from the back to the front, making the PFC the last brain structure to fully develop. For most people, it is not fully developed until they are about 25 years old. Have you heard that young people do not have functioning prefrontal cortexes? Although it may feel like a comfort in explaining some of the odd behaviors seen in classrooms, it is important to remember that the PFC of a young person is already actively engaged in important processing work. That said, because their PFCs are still developing, how that processing works, particularly when it comes to complex decision making and planning skills, is different from adults.

Teachers and families play an important role as students' PFCs develop. Experiences, modeling, and awareness can help children understand their neuroanatomy and build effective developmentally appropriate strategies to reason through challenges.

KEY CONCEPT

Amygdala: An almond-shaped cluster of nuclei located in the temporal lobe. It is associated with emotional responses and memories, particularly responses to stress and fear.

When young people face challenges, the *amygdala* plays an important role in their response. For more information about the role of the amygdala in emotional regulation, see Chapter 7.

Families and teachers are often well-acquainted with the strong emotional responses of young people. It helps to know that there is a neurological reason for this intensity. As students get older, the prefrontal cortex plays an increasing role in helping them process challenging and stressful situations through reason. Along the way, teachers and families can take many steps to support children as their prefrontal cortex is developing (see Figure 7).

FIGURE 7
Strategies to Support Prefrontal Cortex
Development in Young People

- **Model** what it looks like to reason through a challenge or set an action plan to persist toward a goal.
- **Calmly explain cause and effect,** including talking through action/consequences.
- Teach young people about the **functions of the amygdala and the prefrontal cortex.**
- If a young person does something impulsive and tells you they don't know what they were thinking, they are probably telling the truth. They probably weren't thinking as much as they were feeling. **Work with them on strategies to activate the prefrontal cortex.** I often ask young people to identify their emotional/stress/fear/anger triggers (e.g., scratchy throat, tight chest, clenched jaw, sweaty hands, etc.). Young people can begin to associate these triggers with big feelings and view them as a warning that it may be time to activate the prefrontal cortex.
- **Use strength-based language to remind young people that they are resilient.** Remind students of times when they worked through and even overcame difficult things. Celebrate those victories.
- **Encourage young people to come to you with their challenges.** When they do, ask if they want you to just listen so they can be heard or listen and offer guidance so that you can problem solve together. Respect their requests.

All of these strategies help young people form connections within the brain between cause and effect, action and consequence, and plans and goals. In order to start this process, teachers must first get young people's attention. Judy Willis (2006), a neurologist and middle school teacher, wrote that "before students can make memories or learn, something or someone must capture their attention" (p. 38). Chapter 2 discussed the power of an engaging question to capture or direct attention. Other strategies include novelty, surprise, and connecting to students' interest areas. In the following activities, students will explore how unlocking wonder can unleash potential. They will then create independent research projects in defense of daydreaming.

KEY TERMS FOR EDUCATORS

- **Lateral regions:** Toward the side body.
- **Medial regions:** Near the midline of the body.
- **Stimulus-independent and task-unrelated thoughts (SITUT):** Also known as mind-wandering.

Classroom Application

Unit Overview

As students explore that rich space between rational planning and positive daydreaming, this unit is a call to nurture wonder in the classroom. It opens with a springboard text and thought sheet introducing wonder as both a noun and verb. As students explore curious questions, they learn that when they wonder, neurologically they are seeking connections across their brain cell networks, linking a question or topic with all of the other relevant information they have learned about the topic. In the next activity, students move from the abstract to the concrete, as they learn about the prefrontal cortex and complete a series of exercises to activate the PFC. Next, students bring their unique perspectives to a series of four circles. Each circle includes a different prompt asking students to approach it through cartography, math, art, fantasy, and statistics. The "make it stick" assessment for this unit is an independent research project in defense of daydreaming.

Time Suggestions

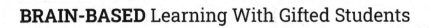

Class 1 (25 minutes)	Class 2 (20 minutes)	Class 3 (30 minutes)	Class 4 (30 minutes)	Extension (variable)
• Handout 4.1: Our Brains Need Wonder • Handout 4.2: Warming Up Our Sense of Wonder • Essential Question and Learning Objectives	• Handout 4.3: A Prefrontal Cortex Workout	• Handout 4.4: One Circle, Four Views	• Handout 4.5: Make It Stick!: In Defense of Daydreaming	• Extending and Transferring the Concept

Name: _____ Date: _____

Sparking Connection With Wonder

Essential Question

- How can you respond to the world with both wonder and reason?

Learning Objectives

By the end of this unit, I will . . .
- consider the role wonder plays in my own life,
- practice strategies to strengthen my developing prefrontal cortex,
- complete an interdisciplinary activity using multiple perspectives, and
- present a project in defense of daydreaming.

HANDOUT 4.1
Our Brains Need Wonder

Have you ever come across something you didn't understand and wanted to know more about? Maybe it was a machine, and you were curious about how it worked. Maybe it was a math problem that had a symbol you hadn't seen before. Maybe it was wanting to help an injured frog or the way your grandmother looked at you when you brought that injured frog into her kitchen.

When you look up at the night sky, do you consider the galaxies millions of light-years away? Have you ever tried to understand how big the ocean is, or wanted to know more about how the moon affects the tides, or wondered why so much of our planet is made of water?

Have you ever asked your family so many questions they grew tired of answering you? Maybe you are curious about the definitions of words, why things work the way they do, whether or not people who go to different houses of worship pray to different gods, who invented the first piano or the first computer, how many people it takes to build a rocket, what it feels like to do a cartwheel on the moon, what happens if you double the butter in your cookie recipe, or how penguins meet their partner. There is a lot to be curious about.

Have you ever stayed up at night worrying about big issues in the world, like poverty and racism?

All of these questions are examples of **wonder**. Wonder leads to what Judy Willis (2006) called "optimal brain activation" (p. 44). Wonder is both a noun and a verb. You might remember that nouns are people, places, or things. Wonder is that feeling of surprise caused by something interesting, beautiful, unexpected, or difficult to explain.

Verbs are action words. When we wonder, we are curious, thinking, considering, and problem solving. We are working things out. Sometimes we are gathering more information, often by asking questions. When we wonder, we are seeking connections across our brain cell networks, linking this question or topic with all of the other relevant information we have learned about the topic. Our world is full of interesting, beautiful, unexpected things, people, and experiences, many of which are difficult to understand and explain.

It is important to wonder, to be curious, to ask questions, to notice, to experiment, and to research. Sometimes you are noticing things in a way that no one has before. Keep wondering!

The world needs thinkers just like you.

Reference

Willis, J. (2006). *Research-based strategies to ignite student learning.* Association for Supervision and Curriculum Development.

HANDOUT 4.1, *continued*

Comprehension and Reflection Questions

1. There are many questions in this handout. Which are the most interesting to you, and why?

   _____

   _____

   _____

   _____

   _____

2. Use the word *wonder* in a sentence. In your sentence, did you use the word as a noun or verb?

   _____

   _____

   _____

   _____

   _____

3. What does this article teach about wonder and the brain? _____

   _____

   _____

   _____

   _____

4. Why do you think the author says the world needs wonder? _____

   _____

   _____

   _____

   _____

Sparking Connection With Wonder

HANDOUT 4.2

Warming Up Our Sense of Wonder

1. What do you wonder about when you are falling asleep? _____

   _____

   _____

   _____

2. What questions do you have about outer space? _____

   _____

   _____

   _____

3. If you could go on a research trip to learn more about any animal in the world, which animal would you choose, and why?

   _____

   _____

   _____

   _____

4. What do you believe is the most important issue for humans to solve in your lifetime?

   _____

   _____

   _____

   _____

5. If you could ask your great-great-grandparents one question, what would you ask them?

   _____

   _____

   _____

   _____

Sparking Connection With Wonder

HANDOUT 4.2, *continued*

6. If you could take a class on anything, what would you want to learn about?

   _____

   _____

   _____

   _____

7. Finish this sentence: *I wish someone would write a book about . . .*

   _____

   _____

   _____

   _____

8. What do you think will be the most important advancements in the next 30 years?

   _____

   _____

   _____

   _____

Sparking Connection With Wonder

HANDOUT 4.3

A Prefrontal Cortex Workout

Often adults tell young people that their prefrontal cortexes aren't yet fully developed. (Gee, thanks.) Although the **prefrontal cortex**, abbreviated PFC, continues to develop throughout your school years and into your mid-20s, it is already doing some amazing and important work. The PFC is an organizer, a decider, and a thinker.

The PFC is the area of the **frontal lobe** that lies directly behind your eyes and forehead. The PFC supports thinking (or **cognitive processes**), organization, memory, attention, and your ability to plan and keep working toward a goal. It receives information and communicates across the brain to help you plan a response.

Thought Exercises to Strengthen Your Developing PFC

1. Think of a great role model who has achieved many of their goals. What specific strategies did they use to reach these goals? If possible, ask this person about their planning and persistence.

   _____

   _____

   _____

   _____

2. There are many examples of cause and effect in science. How do you see cause and effect in your interactions with others and in your own behaviors?

   _____

   _____

   _____

   _____

3. What does the amygdala do? What does the prefrontal cortex do? (*Note.* Additional research encouraged.)

   _____

   _____

   _____

   _____

Sparking Connection With Wonder

HANDOUT 4.3, *continued*

4. What does it look like to activate your prefrontal cortex? What behaviors and strategies do you use when you are planning, reasoning, and organizing?

   _____

   _____

   _____

   _____

5. What are your own emotional, stress, fear, or anger triggers (e.g., scratchy throat, tight chest, clenched jaw, sweaty hands, etc.)?

   _____

   _____

   _____

   _____

6. How can knowing those triggers help you commit to activating the prefrontal cortex?

   _____

   _____

   _____

   _____

7. Remember that you are strong. What are some examples of challenges you have overcome?

   _____

   _____

   _____

   _____

8. Who can you go to for listening or guidance when you have a challenge?

   _____

   _____

   _____

   _____

Sparking Connection With Wonder

HANDOUT 4.4

One Circle, Four Views

Directions: Making meaning requires you to connect ideas and content together. Use the following circles as a starting place to complete the four different activities.

Challenge 1

Pretend this circle is the globe. How much of the Earth can you draw? Include as many continents, oceans, and details as possible.

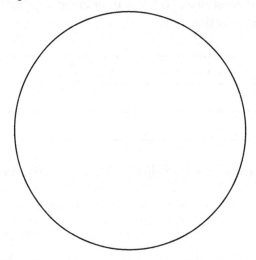

Thought Question: Why is it difficult to draw the entire Earth in this circle? Is there another two-dimensional shape that would better represent the Earth?

Challenge 2

Imagine the inside of this circle is the start of an art project. Finish the drawing.

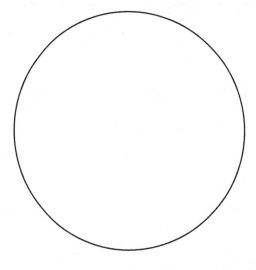

HANDOUT 4.4, *continued*

Challenge 3

Instead of starting with the inside of the circle, start with the *outside*. How does your scene change if you imagine the circle is a window, a hole, or a portal?

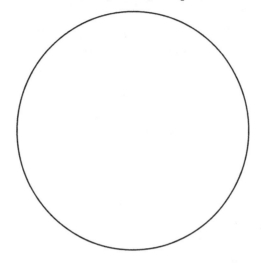

Challenge 4

What if the circle isn't part of a picture in art, but a picture in math? What if the circle is a pie chart? Make a pie chart about your life. (A pie chart is a graph in which a circle is divided into sections that each represent a part of the whole.) You might make a chart about your emotions, your hopes, your worries, the issues you care about, or how you spend your time.

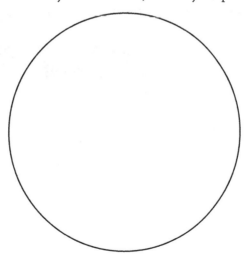

Sparking Connection With Wonder

HANDOUT 4.5

Make It Stick!: In Defense of Daydreaming

WONDER WORDS

Wonder (simplified neuroscience): When you wonder, you are seeking connections across your brain cell networks, linking a question or topic with all of the other relevant information you have learned about the topic.

Wonder (noun): A feeling of surprise caused by something interesting, beautiful, unexpected, or difficult to explain.

Wonder (verb): To be curious; to think about or try to learn more about something interesting.

Challenge: In Defense of Daydreaming

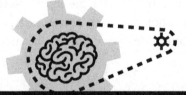

Create a project in defense of daydreaming. Your project should answer this question: *Why is it important to wonder or daydream?* You have a lot of choices in this project in terms of process (how you interpret the question) and product (how you demonstrate your answer). The ideas on the next page will help get you started.

KEY TERMS

Amygdala: An almond-shaped cluster of nuclei located in the temporal lobe; associated with emotional responses and memories, particularly responses to stress and fear.

Persist: To continue toward a goal even when doing so is challenging and the outcome is uncertain.

Prefrontal cortex (PFC): The area of the frontal lobe that lies directly behind the eyes and forehead. It supports cognitive processes, particularly executive function or the ability to plan and persist toward a goal. The PFC is responsible for complex social-emotional and cognitive tasks by receiving information and communicating across the brain to help plan a response.

Sparking Connection With Wonder

HANDOUT 4.5, *continued*

Process: Interpreting the Question
(Choosing a Focus Topic)

- **Neuroscience of daydreaming:** What happens in our brains when we wonder or daydream?
- **Art:** Why do artists (or musicians) need to daydream or wonder?
- **Science:** How has daydreaming and wonder helped advance science?
- **Math:** How could wonder and daydreaming support mathematical thinking?
- **Engineering:** Why do engineers need to wonder and daydream?
- **Personal narrative:** How has wonder and daydreaming helped you?

Product: Demonstrating Your Answer
(Materials and Format)

- Draw a diagram
- Create an infographic
- Write a report
- Make a PowerPoint
- Give a speech
- Author a comic book or graphic novel

Sparking Connection With Wonder

Extending and Transferring the Concept

The activities in this unit offer an entry point for (1) exploring wonder and (2) learning more about brain-positive strategies that respect students' developing prefrontal cortexes. The following are additional suggestions to extend these activities in your classroom.

Handout 4.1: Our Brains Need Wonder

- **Write a wonder manifesto:** Handout 4.1 offers a series of questions to spark curiosity. Challenge students to write their own "wonder manifesto" filled with questions they are curious about. You might also have students review and build on some of their question lists from Chapter 2.
- **Take it a step further:** Once they have completed their wonder manifestos, introduce students to spoken word poetry. Have them revise and then perform their wonder manifestos in a classwide poetry slam.

Handout 4.2: Warming Up Our Sense of Wonder

- **Independent research/authorship:** NAGC Curriculum Planning Standard 3.5 asks that teachers support students with gifts and talents in becoming *independent investigators*. This handout provides a catalyst for independent projects in students' unique interest areas. Ask students to pick a focus question and chase down the answers/solutions through independent research and the creative process.

Handout 4.3: A Prefrontal Cortex Workout

- **Go deeper with neuroanatomy:** This activity gives general information about the prefrontal cortex. Invite a neuroscientist or neurologist to your class to give a guest lecture and answer student questions about the PFC and amygdala.

Handout 4.4: One Circle, Four Views

- **Give more time:** This activity can easily be extended with materials and extra time for students to develop art, science, or math pieces that are more thoughtful and polished. If you want to go deeper with this activity but don't have the time to extend all four circles, have students complete the activity as written and then choose one circle to develop more fully. Host a gallery walk of their final products and end with a classwide discussion. The following are some starter questions for this dialogue:
  - What does this activity teach you about perspective?
  - Why did you choose that particular circle to develop more fully?
  - What did you learn about science, math, or art in completing this activity?
  - What surprised and impressed you in viewing your classmates' work?

Handout 4.5: Make It Stick!: *In Defense of Daydreaming*

- **Student seminar:** Given the wide latitude in process and product, these projects could be used to create a dynamic student-led seminar. Student-led showcases and seminars are powerful ways to make classroom learning more visible to the broader community. Invite families and other classes to learn more about students' work and thinking on positive constructive daydreaming.

Additional Extensions

The ways educators can encourage wonder, monitor meaning-making, and create space for productive mind-wandering are expansive. The following are several ideas to help transfer these concepts beyond the activities in this unit.

- **Wonder interviews with content experts:** Host expert panels and guest talks with diverse content experts. Across these talks, ask how wonder, mind-wandering, and positive constructive daydreaming have influenced their work and practice. Potential questions include:
  - How has wonder influenced your work?
  - What do you wonder about professionally and personally?
  - Can you think of a time when mind-wandering helped you or a coworker come up with a great idea? How can people use mind-wandering or daydreaming for good?

▪ In class we learned about the work of Jerome Singer, who said that some daydreaming is both positive and constructive. What do you think about that? What examples of positive constructive daydreaming have you seen in your own work?

Content experts may include outside-of-school professionals, such as mathematicians, scientists, artists, musicians, etc., and inside-of-school professionals, such as core and elective teachers, administrators, and support staff. Throughout your practice, demonstrate to students that everyone has wisdom to offer (see Chapter 5 on social cognition).

■ **Activate the prefrontal cortex:** Help students use neuroanatomical language, including *activate my prefrontal cortex*. In order for this phrase to be meaningful, students need both some prior knowledge of the PFC and opportunities to brainstorm what it looks like to organize, reason, plan, and persist. As you develop this common language, students can begin to associate activating their prefrontal cortex with activities such as problem solving, goal setting, and responding to stress. Figure 8 is a thought sheet students can use to begin thinking about what it means to activate the prefrontal cortex. You can also make a classwide anchor chart on this topic that you coauthor throughout the year.

■ **Neuroscience lab field trip:** If you are following the lessons in this book in order, your students have now had lots of exposure to neuroanatomy concepts. If possible, this would be a great time to arrange a field trip to a neuroscience lab. In preparation for the field trip, students should review their brain diagrams, as well as the key terms, such as *prefrontal cortex* and *amygdala*. Students should also think about the neuroscience research questions they think would be interesting or important to explore and bring these ideas to the lab when they visit.

FIGURE 8
Thought Sheet: Activate the PFC

Name:

ACTIVATE THE PFC

The Prefrontal Cortex (PFC) is the area of the frontal lobe that lies directly behind the eyes and forehead. It is important for cognitive processes, particularly executive function or the ability to plan and persist toward a goal.

What does it look like to organize, plan, and persist toward a goal?

Organize: _____

Plan: _____   *Persist:* _____

Over time, we want to associate activating the prefrontal cortex with activities such as problem-solving tasks, goal setting, and responding to stress.

Chapter 5

Social Cognition

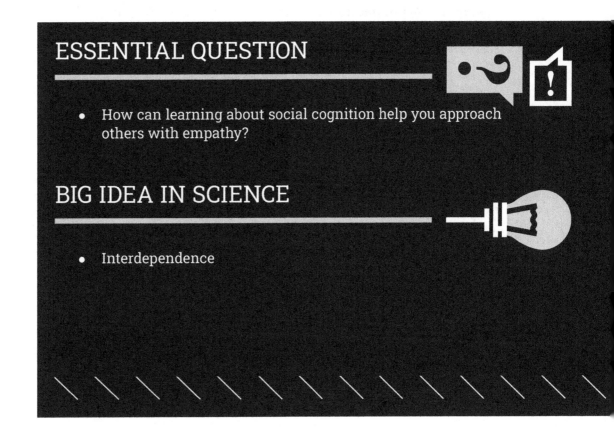

ESSENTIAL QUESTION

- How can learning about social cognition help you approach others with empathy?

BIG IDEA IN SCIENCE

- Interdependence

Seeking Social Connection for Gifted Brains

The Interpersonal Connection model encourages gifted youth to consider the feelings and experiences of others and to approach people with wonder. This framework asks students to identify the many communities to which they belong and reflect on how those communities impact them as well as how they impact their communities. Through leveraging the *cognitive triangle* (connecting one's thoughts, behaviors, and feelings), this model helps students think differently about relationships. Interpersonal Connection activities, such as those outlined in this chapter, play to gifted children's cognitive propensity for connection while also offering new approaches to make sense of and think about relationships.

KEY CONCEPT

Interpersonal Connection model: A metacognitive teaching model that uses what is known about social cognition to foster empathy, understanding, and relationship building.

Learning Through Connection to Others

Neuroscientists and psychologists study social cognition to explore how they perceive, remember, and respond to others. In his book on human cognition, Tomasello (1999) wrote, "Human beings [have] a single very special form of social cognition, namely, the ability of individual organisms to understand conspecifics [those within the species] as beings like themselves who have intentional and mental lives like their own" (p. 5). Said differently, people have the unique ability to know about their own minds and the minds of others, and then to make connections between how these different minds work together. These connections lead to new types of knowledge.

KEY CONCEPT

Social cognition: The unique ways that people are able to share knowledge, learn together and about each other, and use this information to inform and inspire their own thinking.

Neuroscientists have shown that the way people connect with others is critical to how they learn, particularly how they learn about themselves. Self-knowledge is not sensory as much as it is motor (Adolphs, 2009). People know about the things they can share with others. People can understand themselves and others as conscious beings with unique thought processes (Frith & Frith, 2007). Interpersonal Connection guides students in acting on that realization with wonder, empathy, and a thirst for learning. Leveraging social cognition gives humans the ability to forge new connections, take action, and practice agency.

Empathy, or the ability to mentally put oneself in the position of others in order to understand and respond with compassion, has been linked to a particular cluster of cells called *mirror neurons*. Marco Iacoboni (2008), a neuroscientist at UCLA, advanced the understanding of these important cells located in the premotor cortex and inferior parietal cortex. These cells are activated when a person performs an action such as smiling. However, they are also equally activated when observing someone else performing the same action. Iacoboni's work has shown the important link between mirror neurons and social cognition. His work has also led to studies on how changes in mirror neurons may be present in people with autism and others with differently wired brains.

NEUROANATOMICAL TIDBIT

Mirror neurons: A cluster of cells that fire both when a person executes a motor act (e.g., smiling) and when they observe another individual performing the same or a similar motor act. Mirror neurons are located in the premotor cortex, the supplementary motor area, the primary somatosensory cortex, and the inferior parietal cortex (Acharya & Shukla, 2012).

The Interpersonal Connection Model

The Interpersonal Connection model (see Figure 9) begins with students reflecting on their own lived experience as a story. The story frame is a familiar starting place for young students. Students can recognize that stories have many characters, and in the story of their life, they are the protagonist. Thinking of themselves as protagonists gives young children agency in much the same way that practicing metacognition puts them in charge of their own thinking. Next, students consider some of the different communities to which they belong and then sort or code these into categories. These activities give students a cast of meaningful characters that they are connected to.

Having brainstormed different people in their lives, students then analyze how their relationships with others influence their thoughts and feelings. Asking students the following questions supports this inquiry:

- Who inspires you?
- Who includes you?
- Whom do you adore?
- Whom do you learn from?

The nuance among terms like *inspire*, *adore*, and *include* may be new for young children, and so teachers will want to define these in a continued effort to build emotional vocabulary.

I use Interpersonal Connection as a brain-based model to help students think about their relationships to others and how these relationships impact their thinking. The next layer of the model gives students a developmentally appropriate way to introduce social cognition by reflecting on a key idea that wisdom is ubiquitous. Students are asked to identify an everyday sage who makes a positive difference in their lives. After identifying this individual, they then write and deliver a thank you card to their everyday sage.

Having identified and reflected on many positive relationships in their lives, students next turn their attention to difficult relationships. Again, they are using their own lived experiences as a curriculum in how they can (and do) interact with others. This time students reflect on how they interact with people who annoy them, make them mad, or "push their buttons." This is an opportunity to (1) talk explicitly about empathy, a trait that gifted students often excel in, and (2) reinforce the concept of wisdom being ubiquitous. Class discussion can include candid remarks about how human interaction is both essential and challenging. The following lesson offers a "listening + action" strategy for students to use in navigating these difficult situations. This is also an opportunity to introduce the role of mirror neurons and to practice mirroring. To scaffold this strategy, students

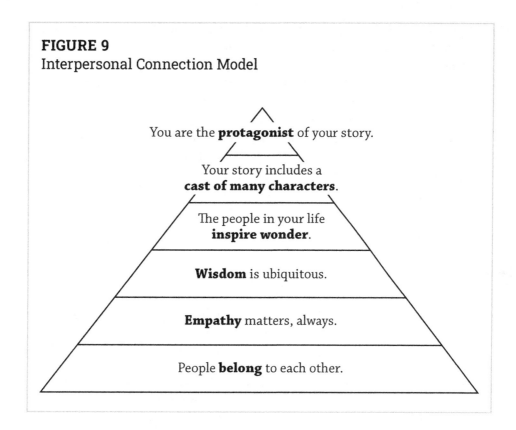

FIGURE 9
Interpersonal Connection Model

You are the **protagonist** of your story.

Your story includes a
cast of many characters.

The people in your life
inspire wonder.

Wisdom is ubiquitous.

Empathy matters, always.

People **belong** to each other.

practice a physical mirroring activity before practicing a storytelling exchange between peers.

This chapter's activities challenge students to (1) recognize the sages in their lives and respond with gratitude, (2) reach out to diverse communities with the understanding that everyone has wisdom to offer, and (3) navigate difficult exchanges with empathy.

Social-Emotional Challenges for Gifted Youth

Gifted youth present with many unique thinking, feeling, and doing processes, which are sometimes in conflict with other brains in the school building. The social-emotional needs and challenges of gifted youth are well-documented in the literature. To summarize the important work of many scholars in this field: Nurturing the complex needs of gifted youth requires careful instruction that appropriately challenges, adequately supports, and honors the uniquely individualized profiles of students who may be different from their peers. Gifted children often experience *social asynchrony*. For example, a second-grade gifted student may read high school-level texts yet still struggle with turn taking and sharing. The purpose of social skills instruction for gifted students should not be to make these young people more like everyone else, but to help these students find belonging, acceptance, and connection within their school communities. In a review of peer relationships for gifted and highly gifted youth, Lovecky (1995) put it this way: "The goal is not to make the highly gifted child conform to peer expectations, but to help the child develop adequate social skills to support cognitive and emotional needs. Without appropriate intervention, social difficulties are likely to be lifelong" (para. 13). The stakes are high. Teachers are tasked with helping children develop the skills to experience success, joy, and belonging in the classroom and beyond.

KEY CONCEPT

Social asynchrony: Uneven patterns of academic and social development common among gifted learners.

There is often a mismatch between the school environment and the needs of gifted students. Finding appropriate instruction for gifted and highly gifted youth that meets students where they are socially, emotionally, and cognitively requires extensive creativity, intervention, and flexibility within the school schedule. Many schools do not have the training, structure, or resources to deliver this kind of comprehensive and varied instruction. This often means that gifted teachers and coordinators, or others in the school building with a passion for gifted and talented youth, have to step in and propose creativity, intervention, and flexibility.

Returning to the example of the second-grade gifted student who is reading high school-level texts but struggling with turn taking and sharing, it is easy to see how this youth may have trouble finding a true friend, sometimes called a *true peer*. The kids with her emotional maturity do not share her academic interests, and the students with her academic interests are in a different social-emotional place than she is. Gifted youth often need many diverse peers with whom they can build different kinds of relationships and friendships. This can translate into an opportunity for direct teaching about the importance of diversity. The ways that teachers talk about, honor, and invite diversity help build culturally responsive classrooms that both meet students' needs and prepare them to live and learn in a diverse world.

The activities shared in this chapter help students explore these concepts directly, talk about them in the safety of their class communities, and set specific goals and intentions to become more proficient collaborators and communicators.

KEY TERMS FOR EDUCATORS

- **Cognitive triangle:** Connecting one's thoughts, behaviors, and feelings.
- **Empathy:** The ability to mentally put oneself in the position of others in order to understand and respond with compassion.
- **Emotional vocabulary:** Knowing different words to describe feelings with nuance and specificity.

Classroom Application

Unit Overview

This unit guides students through a series of scaffolded Interpersonal Connection activities. Through these activities, students consider how they are members of communities, how members of communities are related, how others might be feeling in a situation, and how they can approach everyone with wonder. This model plays to gifted children's cognitive propensity for connection by giving them new ways to think about and approach relationships. The unit concludes with the authoring of a community-wide pledge outlining students' commitments to learn together.

Time Suggestions

Class 1 (30 minutes)	Class 2 (40 minutes)	Class 3 (20 minutes)	Class 4 (30 minutes)	Extension (variable)
• Handout 5.1: The Characters in Our Lives • Essential Question and Learning Objectives	• Handout 5.2: Approaching People With Wonder • Handout 5.3: Wisdom Is Ubiquitous	• Handout 5.4: Mirroring: Responding With Empathy	• Handout 5.5: Make It Stick!: Social Cognition	• Extending and Transferring the Concept

STUDENT ACTIVITIES

Social Cognition

Essential Question

- How can learning about social cognition help you approach others with empathy?

Learning Objectives

By the end of this unit, I will . . .

- consider the characters in my life;
- brainstorm the people who inspire me, as well as the people I admire, adore, and learn from;
- learn about social cognition and the idea that wisdom is ubiquitous;
- write a thank you letter to an everyday sage who makes a positive difference in my life;
- practice a strategy called mirroring to approach difficult interactions with empathy; and
- think about what my relationships with others can teach me about thinking and wisdom.

HANDOUT 5.1

The Characters in Our Lives

In literature, characters are the people, creatures, or figures in a story. In books, we find characters we love and admire and characters whose choices we disagree with and even dislike. Characters tend to either earn our trust or mistrust. In literature, the **main character** or **protagonist** is the character who leads the action. Sometimes we think of this character as the hero.

Our own lives are also made up of many characters. Some people we interact with only briefly, like the clerk in the checkout line at the grocery store. Other people we see every day, like the school bus driver who remembers everyone's birthday. Some people teach us such important lessons that we are not quite the same after knowing them.

The teacher who taught you how to read might come to mind. You have people who make you laugh and people with whom you cry. There are people in your families, your neighborhoods, your schools, and your communities. All of these characters impact *your* story.

That's right, this is your story. In the journey of your life, you are the protagonist. Your thoughts, actions, and beliefs drive your story forward and are also influenced by the thoughts, actions, and beliefs of others. In fact, being able to recognize and appreciate the ways your thoughts can work together with those of others is a uniquely human process. In this activity, you will explore the people who make your lived experiences more interesting. You will also learn how you can approach everyone you meet with wonder.

Concentric Circles Activity

Concentric shapes share the same center point. In this activity, map characters in your life. This means that you are that center point. Moving from your smaller communities (e.g., family) to your larger communities (e.g., city), focus on people who have the greatest impact on you.

Name: _____ Date: _____

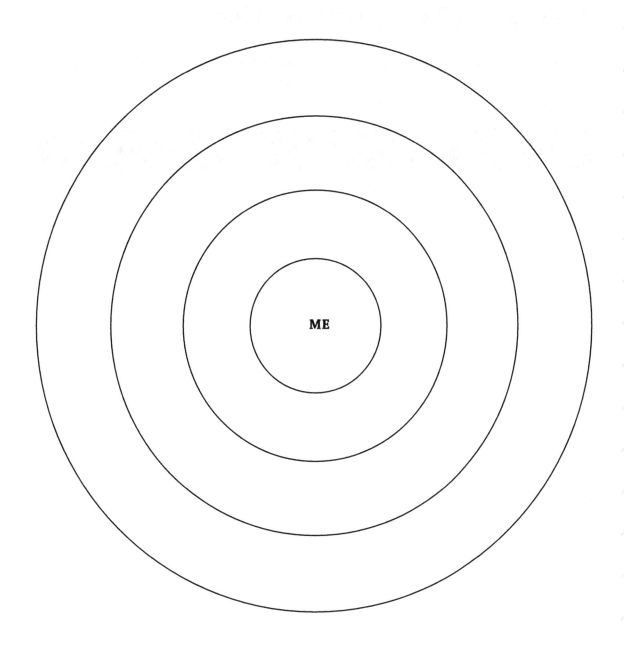

HANDOUT 5.2

Approaching People With Wonder

Directions: A beautiful sunset or the energy of a terrific thunderstorm can fill us with wonder. Just as we find wonder in the natural world, we can also approach people with wonder. Using the following chart, reflect on the different people in your own life.

Who inspires you?	Who includes you?	Whom do you adore?	Whom do you learn from?
When you are inspired by someone, you feel like you can accomplish great things.	*When you are included, you feel like you belong and are welcome.*	*When you adore someone, you love and respect them and want to keep them safe.*	*Think about the people who have taught you something new.*

HANDOUT 5.2, *continued*

Comprehension and Reflection Questions

1. What can the people on your list teach you about thinking?_____

_____

_____

_____

_____

2. Do you think your school is inclusive of students who learn differently? Why or why not?

_____

_____

_____

_____

_____

3. How can your school be more inclusive?_____

_____

_____

_____

_____

Social Cognition

Name: _____ Date: _____

Wisdom Is Ubiquitous

When you think of the people who inspire wonder and wisdom, who comes to mind?
- Your teachers?
- Experts?
- Famous people?

Sure! Nobel Peace Prize winners, Olympic athletes, energetic third-grade teachers, and award-winning musicians are all certainly inspiring.

However, so are the custodians who keep your school clean, the kind woman who serves lunch in the cafeteria, your older neighbor who has seen more than 90 years of history, the friend who gives you a hug when you are sad, and the student who moved here from another country and is teaching you phrases in Vietnamese. Through this activity, you may start to see that wisdom is **ubiquitous**, or all around. Everywhere you pay attention, there is something to learn. Everyone you meet has wisdom to offer and lessons to teach.

Neuroscience has shown us that humans have the unique ability to learn more when we pool our collective wisdom. This is a special phenomenon called **social cognition**. One way to strengthen our social connection is to connect with the real people in our lives.

Challenge

Directions: Think of an **everyday sage** who inspires wonder or wisdom in your life (a sage is someone who has gained wisdom). This person likely makes a positive difference to the people around them. Write them a thank you letter today. Use the following chart to help you plan and format your letter.

Date
Write today's date
(Month/date/year)

Salutation,
Options: *Dear, Hi,* or *Good morning* + the name of the person to whom you are writing

Body
Include several thoughtful sentences with clear examples. For this letter, you will want to explain why the person you are writing to makes a positive difference in your life and inspires wonder.

Closing
Options: *Sincerely, Warmly,* or *Your friend* + your signature

Social Cognition

Brain-Based Learning With Gifted Students © Prufrock Press Inc.

HANDOUT 5.4

Mirroring: Responding With Empathy

We have talked about appreciating wonder in the people who inspire us. We have talked about honoring wonder in the people we admire and adore. What about the people who aren't easy to get along with? What about the people who annoy us, push our buttons, or make us mad? Is it important to approach them with wonder, too? Of course, it is! Remember, everyone has something to teach us. Although we all have different ways of showing it, everyone also wants to love and be loved.

When we are interacting with people who are difficult for us, we can challenge ourselves to use empathy to see their point of view. **Empathy** is being able to consider and relate to someone's else's feelings.

The next time someone bothers you, try to see things from their point of view. If you are arguing, seek to find a middle path together. When you are listening to someone who annoys you, try to really listen. It is not easy. However, because you are ultimately in charge of your actions and thoughts, you can make important decisions about how you respond to others.

Our brains have a cluster of important cells, called **mirror neurons**, that help us see our experiences in the experiences of others. By understanding others' feelings and thoughts, we can choose to respond with empathy.

The following practice activities on **mirroring** will help you begin to develop these skills.

Mirroring Activity

Directions: Work with a partner to complete these challenges.

Challenge 1

One person is the conductor, and the other is the mirror. Facing each other, the mirror should perfectly copy the movements of the conductor. If the conductor stretches their arms out into a T, the mirror stretches their arms out into a T. As you continue to play the game, you might try harder poses, such as standing on one leg. After 1–2 minutes, switch roles.

Challenge 2

Working in the same pairs, assign new roles. This time, one person is the storyteller, and the other mirror. The storyteller thinks about a time when they were mad, sad, or frustrated. Then, the storyteller shares the story of this memory, pausing after every sentence or two. When the storyteller pauses, the mirror repeats what they heard. For example, if the storyteller said, "I was already having a terrible day. Then, I got home, and my mom said, 'We need to talk,'" the mirror would say, "You were having a terrible day, and then your mom wanted to talk to you." The mirror can use the exact same words or slightly different words. This challenge isn't about memorizing,

Social Cognition

but about paying attention and trying to understand, which are exercises in empathy. After 2–4 minutes, switch roles.

Comprehension and Reflection Questions

1. What was difficult about this activity? Why was it difficult?

   _____

   _____

   _____

   _____

2. In your own words, what is empathy? _____

   _____

   _____

   _____

   _____

3. How can mirroring help you approach people with more empathy?

   _____

   _____

   _____

   _____

Social Cognition

Brain-Based Learning With Gifted Students © Prufrock Press Inc.

Name: _____ Date: _____

Make It Stick!: Social Cognition

Challenge: Social Cognition, A Community Pledge

Write a community-wide pledge on social cognition. Your pledge should include the following:

- An introduction to your community and this project.
  - Required: Define *social cognition* and *empathy*.
  - Optional: Define *mirror neurons* and *inclusion*.

- A list of specific commitments for how your community (e.g., small group, class, family) will commit to learning *with* your broader communities (e.g., class, school, city). Include at least eight specific commitments. Commitments should be positively stated. You will need to practice collaborative skills to gain consensus and coauthor this pledge.
- A conclusion that describes the importance of maintaining this pledge.

Prominently display your pledge in your classroom (or home) and revisit it often.

> **KEY TERMS**
>
> **Characters:** The people, creatures, or figures in a story.
>
> **Protagonist:** The main character who leads the story or action.
>
> **Concentric circles:** Circles that share the same center point.
>
> **Ubiquitous:** Everywhere.
>
> **Social cognition:** How groups of people can think and learn together.
>
> **Mirror neurons:** A cluster of cells in the brain that help people practice empathy.
>
> **Consensus:** Agreement among a group.

SOCIAL-EMOTIONAL VOCABULARY

Trust: Belief in the ability, strength, or reliability of someone or something.

Inspire: To cause one to feel like they can accomplish great things.

Adore: To love, respect, and care for someone.

Include/Inclusion: To welcome and let others know that they belong.

Empathy: The ability to consider and relate to someone's else's feelings.

Mirroring: Imitating the movements or speech of another person, often as an act of empathy.

Extending and Transferring the Concept

Great teaching begins in relationships. Neuroscience teaches that great learning also begins in relationships. Many of the social skills teachers focus on in schools, including collaboration, active listening, clear communication, inclusion, empathy, and respect, can be strengthened by lessons on social cognition and mirroring. Interpersonal Connection gives both teachers and students a framework to develop better strategies to learn with and within school communities.

Handout 5.1: The Characters in Our Lives

- **Draw a comic:** What does it mean to be the protagonist of your own story? Have students create a comic to answer this question.
- **Concentric circles at school:** Working in small groups, ask students to reflect on the concentric circles in their school and local communities. Facilitate a conversation about the interconnected world. Ask students how they can better appreciate the people in different communities.

Handout 5.2: Approaching People With Wonder

- **More columns:** Have students create columns with additional positive adjectives or descriptions. For example: *Who makes you laugh? Who gives great advice? Who makes you feel safe?*

Handout 5.3: Wisdom Is Ubiquitous

- **Wisdom celebration:** In addition to writing thank you letters, invite guests to come to a class wisdom celebration. At the celebration, each student should introduce their guest and share what they have learned from them and why they decided to invite this guest.
- **Guest visits:** Use the thank you letters to organize expert guest visits with people in your local community. During these visits guests should be invited to share their professional or personal wisdom. For example, if a student writes to a cafeteria worker, invite that person to your class to share about their work around food preparation and mitigating food insecurity, to share more about their culture, or to do a read aloud. Reinforce that students live in a community of many experts.

Handout 5.4: Mirroring: *Responding With Empathy*

- **Act it out:** Either give students scenarios to role-play or help students write their own scenarios in which using mirroring could help calm an argument. After some rehearsal time, have students perform their skits for the class and then discuss how mirroring might help in their next tense conversation.
- **Teach others:** Organize a lesson in which your class teaches younger students about mirroring and the importance of active listening.

Handout 5.5: Make It Stick!: *Social Cognition*

- **Variations on the pledge:** Have students write the pledge as a rap or spoken word piece. You can also help young people use and develop graphic design skills to create a graphically appealing poster of your pledge. Canva, a cloud-based design software, has several free templates that students can use to develop posters and infographics.

Additional Extension

- **Social cognition goal board:** In the classroom, educators often write goals that are (1) academically focused and (2) only shared between a student/family and teacher. These goals matter. However, you can also cultivate a different kind of goal-writing process that honors what you have learned about social cognition and puts it into practice. The social cognition goal board gives students space to report on the progress and challenges they find in working and learning together. Students can author their own goals and share them on the board. Sticky notes work well for this. As a class you could also choose to write some community-wide goals related to your community pledge (see Handout 5.5). By sharing openly and honestly, class communities become stronger. As you set up the social cognition goal board, you may also choose to have students define key terms from this unit and display those as a header or border. The visual cue may help reinforce key concepts. *Note.* It is important to respect confidentiality on this bulletin board by not listing the names of specific people.

Chapter 6

Neuroplasticity

ESSENTIAL QUESTION

- What factors influence your developing brain, and how can you use this information to grow as a thinker and problem solver?

BIG IDEAS IN SCIENCE

- Structure and Function
- Stability and Change

Unlocking the Potential of Brain Plasticity

Although terms like *neuroplasticity* and *growth mindset* have become more commonplace in classrooms, many teachers still have a lot to learn about how plasticity works in the brain and what exactly it means for teaching practices. This chapter sheds light on how experience and environment affect the brain and why this matters for teaching and learning.

An early breakthrough in understanding neuroplasticity emerged from Eric Kandel's studies in the 1970s on giant marine snails called aplysia (The Nobel Prize, n.d.). Mollusks, such as snails, are invertebrates with simple nervous systems and soft, unsegmented bodies. Kandel chose the aplysia to study because they have a small number of cells that are quite enlarged and easy to see. He found that as aplysia learned, the synapses, or chemical structures between their cells also changed. Kandel discovered that chemical synapses, from those few enlarged mollusk cells to the complex networks of the human brain, all exhibit plasticity or malleability and that these changes are significant in how people learn and also form memories. In 2000, he was awarded a Nobel Prize in Medicine for his discoveries, which laid the foundation for research in neuroplasticity (Doidge, 2016).

KEY CONCEPTS

- **Neuroplasticity:** The ability of the brain to reorganize, grow, and adapt based on experience and environmental factors.
- **Functional plasticity:** The ability of the brain to move functions from an area of the brain that has been damaged to an undamaged area.
- **Structural plasticity:** The ability of the brain to change its physical (and synaptic) structure as a result of learning and experience (Cherry, 2019).

The brain is a continuous, malleable work in progress. It develops and adapts based on genetics, environment, and experience. Because both one's environment and experiences change over the course of the lifetime, so does one's brain. There is evidence that even gene expression can be altered by environment and experience. Therefore, educators have a terrific responsibility to create environments and experiences that cultivate learning and development. In a paper on early experiences and gene expression, the National Scientific Council on the Developing Child at Harvard University (2010) wrote:

> Policymakers can use this knowledge to inform decisions about the allocation of resources for interventions that affect the life circumstances of young children—knowing that effective interventions can literally alter how children's genes work and, thereby, have long-lasting effects on their mental and physical health, learning, and behavior. In this respect, the epigenome is the crucial link between the external environments that shape our experiences and the genes that guide our development. (p. 2)

Plasticity and other adaptive characteristics of the human brain have important implications for classroom practice, including how educators think about teaching and learning.

Neurologically speaking, the primary plastic changes occur in the synapses of brain circuits. *Synapses* are the spaces between cells where connections and information transfer through a process called *neurotransmission* (Mishra et al., 2013). At the neurological level, Willis (2006) suggested that "learning consists of reinforcing the connections between neurons" (p. 14). As people amass experiences, make connections, and rehearse new skills, brain plasticity reshapes and reorganizes neural connections.

Be wary of fixed mindset beliefs, such as the idea that there are critical periods of growth, and if a certain skill isn't learned during these critical periods, then that skill can't be learned. The truth is that brains continue learning and making new connections throughout the lifetime. Although plasticity occurs throughout the lifetime, in young children—particularly very young children—brains are almost continuously engaged in plasticity processes (Mishra et al., 2013). Neuroscience studies suggest that these early experiences play a significant role. However, rather than thinking of these times as the only times people can learn, it's more accurate to think of these early years as *sensitive periods* for brain development (Tibke, 2019, p. 20).

Elementary teachers have a tremendous responsibility and opportunity to help cultivate neural connections that will continue developing into adulthood. As a child grows, so do their neurons, and in turn, their cortex gets thicker (particularly in the elementary years). Then, as the brain prunes underused neurons and dendrites (in the teen years), the cortex gets thinner. Over time, the nerve-signal responses become faster and more efficient (Sousa, 2009; Willis, 2006). Although this process happens to all children as they develop, some studies have suggested that the rate of change is greater in gifted and high-IQ youth (Sousa, 2009, p. 11).

Classroom and home environments play an important role as children's brains are developing. Neuroimaging studies show that positive and supportive learning environments and interventions can positively alter the brain (Carraway, 2014). Likewise, negative experiences, including physical and emotional trauma, also have long-lasting effects in the brain. The recent growth of *trauma-informed instruction* builds on some of these findings. Classroom culture can have a profound impact on learning and social-emotional development, and these impacts reverberate into the synapses of students' brains. See Figure 10 for four brain-based commitments for cultivating healthy classroom culture.

Neuroplasticity can help teachers reframe their perspective on learning expectations. Given that the brain adapts, builds new connections, and reorganizes, teachers can neither know nor predict the limits of a specific student's potential (Tibke, 2019, p. 20). Therefore, they must operate out of a position of both hope and high expectations (Fishman-Weaver, 2019). Two vetted classroom approaches to cultivating neuroplasticity are *growth mindset* and *mental contrasting*.

Growth Mindset

Have you ever heard a student (or worse, a teacher) say something like, "Oh, he just doesn't have a brain for math"? By contrast, have you ever walked into one of those magical classrooms run by perseverance and encouragement, where the teacher fiercely believes that anyone can learn just about anything with enough practice? These examples represent two different beliefs about mindsets. The first, that some people are simply "wired for math" and others are not, represents a fixed mindset. The second, that with enough practice anyone can learn just about anything, represents a growth mindset.

KEY CONCEPT

Growth mindset: Carol Dweck's (2006/2016) applied theory on achievement and learning based on nurturing persistence and process while celebrating challenge and resilience.

FIGURE 10
Brain-Based Commitments for Healthy Classroom Culture

Safe
- Create physically and emotionally safe places to learn.

Inclusive
- Affirm all identities, experiences, and ideas.

Challenging
- Use engaging and relevant curriculum.
- Practice high expectations.

Curious
- Encourage questioning, experimenting, and creating.
- Nurture wonder.

Although everyone has times when they slip into a fixed mindset, neuroscience has shown that the brain can continue to reorganize (and grow) synaptic connections and that educators can harness this property to help students learn at deeper levels. This is the basis for Dweck's (2006/2016) research on helping students (and adults) lead more successful lives. The brain's capacity to adapt to its emotional and physical environment and experiences may be one of the most important brain characteristics for classroom practices.

Dweck's (2006/2016) *Mindset* took schools and classrooms by storm. Growth mindset started showing up in lesson plans, bulletin boards, and staff professional development. However, Dweck (2015) cautioned that in this frenzy to celebrate growth mindset, educators may have missed some essential points:

> Too often nowadays, praise is given to students who are putting forth effort, but *not learning*, in order to make them feel good in the moment: "Great effort! You tried your best!" It's good that the students tried, but it's not good that they're not learning. (para. 6)

She continued to say that truly understanding growth mindset requires wrestling with challenges, and seeking new strategies and approaches when the first one (or seven) don't work. In order for growth mindset approaches to be fruitful in the classroom, teachers need to create environments where it is safe for students to make mistakes and where they receive support to learn from those mistakes.

Mental Contrasting

A talented school counselor I worked with used to introduce mental contrasting by asking students and teachers if they had heard the saying, "If you dream it, you can achieve it"? He would then explain that Gabriele Oettingen, a motivational psychologist, believed that the notion that dreaming alone leads to achievement has some significant limitations. Oettingen's research (Oettingen et al., 2009) showed that if dreaming is the first step in a more strategic goal-setting plan, then it can put individuals on the path to achieving. However, this achievement won't come without honesty, work, and a metacognitive model called *mental contrasting* (Duckworth et al., 2013).

KEY CONCEPT

Mental contrasting: A metacognitive model to link a desired future with the present reality.

Mental contrasting involves visualizing both goals (wishes) and challenges (obstacles) to develop action plans that work (Oettingen et al., 2009). Oettingen developed a helpful acronym to help students and adults practice mental contrasting: WOOP (wish, outcome, obstacle, plan). See Figure 11 for an explanation of the model.

For example, a gifted third-grade student I worked with shared that her wish was to start a pottery business. She had a pinch pot design she was proud of, had been making miniature pots for her friends and family, and now wanted to turn her hobby into a business. Two primary obstacles we discussed were access to more materials and a distribution and marketing plan that her parents would approve of. In the WOOP strategy, every obstacle requires its own plan. In this example, we explored using her birthday and Christmas money as a startup fund or asking her first set of customers to pay upfront for her pottery work. For a marketing plan, we brainstormed that she could create advertisements that her mom could post on social media. The student decided to check with her older brother to see if he could help with delivery of the pots.

The pottery business problem is a high-meaning and interdisciplinary problem. How often are students asked to identify and solve these sorts of problems in the classroom? Often in the general classroom, gifted youth are not taught in their zone of proximal development. This means that gifted youth are given fewer opportunities to stretch into new cognitive realms. Therefore, when they

FIGURE 11
WOOP: Metacognitive Model for Mental Contrasting

W Wish	WOOP starts with identifying a wish. Think of this as being grounded in the power of wonder. As you work with students on identifying wishes, remind them that WOOP only works with goals that are within their sphere of influence. These can and should still be stretch goals, but they can't require bending the rules of time or space.
O Outcome	Once your students have identified a wish, ask them to describe the outcome. What will it look like and feel to like to achieve that goal or when that wish comes true?
O Obstacle	The next step is identifying obstacles. This is where contrasting comes in. This step requires honest work around the obstacles standing between a student and achieving their wish. Help students be specific about the obstacles they will face in achieving their wish. Model an open conversation about this for the class.
P Plan	Finally, for each obstacle students identify, help them develop a plan to overcome that obstacle. Together these plans provide clear and targeted direction to making wishes come true.

Note. Strategy adapted from Oettingen et al. (2009).

experience challenging classroom tasks, this feeling may be unfamiliar, and they may have few strategies to persist through these challenges. Directly teaching concepts such as neuroplasticity, growth mindset, and mental contrasting can help gifted students not only approach challenges with interest but also seek them as a way to grow.

KEY CONCEPT

Zone of proximal development: Developed by psychologist Lev Vygotsky, the zone of proximal development (ZPD) refers to the difference between what a learner can do without help and what they can achieve with the guidance of a more knowledgeable other. This requires giving students "interesting and culturally meaningful learning and problem-solving tasks that are slightly more difficult than what [they can] do alone" (Shabani et al., 2010, p. 238). By working through these scaffolded processes, Vygotsky believed educators could continue to raise students' ZPDs. This notion is directly related to what neuroscientists have shown regarding brain plasticity.

Educators have tools to help students take control of their behaviors and can create plans and habits that help them learn new skills. With the right combination of effort and circumstances, they can even achieve their dreams. One of the ways to cultivate neuroplasticity in classrooms is by helping students contrast where they are now and where they want to be, and encouraging them that they can persist over the challenges in between (Fishman-Weaver, 2019). Teaching students about neuroplasticity is an empowering lesson in anatomy and agency.

KEY TERMS FOR EDUCATORS

- **Dendrites:** The branches of a neuron that conduct impulses toward the cell.

- **Epigenetics:** An area of study that shows how environmental factors influence the expression of genes.

- **Neurogenesis**: The growth and development of nervous tissue, specifically the process by which new neurons are grown in the brain.

- **Synapses:** The space between cells where messages are delivered through a process called neurotransmission.

- **Trauma-informed instruction:** Educational practices, particularly in social-emotional learning that seek to support students affected by trauma and respond to their needs with research-based strategies.

Classroom Application

Unit Overview

The following unit gives students opportunities to explore neuroplasticity, or the ability of the brain to reorganize (and grow) synaptic connections. Building on synapse science, students learn about the anatomy of the neuron. Next, students engage with unit vocabulary and growth mindset phrases, including positive thinking self-talk through a bingo game. Afterward, students practice mental contrasting, using the WOOP model (Oettingen et al., 2009). The concluding challenge for this unit asks students to more deeply explore the contributions of one of the researchers introduced in the following activities. In addition to research and presentation skills, students are also asked to connect why these scientific discoveries matter in their own lives at a personal level. By the end of this unit, students should know that the human brain is the product of genes, experiences, and environment. Further, they should learn strategies to persist through challenges with the knowledge that the choices they make affect their continuously developing brains.

Time Suggestions

Class 1 (20 minutes)	Class 2 (20 minutes)	Class 3 (25 minutes)	Class 4 (40 minutes)	Extension (variable)
• Handout 6.1: Neuroplasticity • Essential Question and Learning Objectives	• Handout 6.2: Synapse Science	• Handout 6.3: Growth Mindset Bingo • Handout 6.4. Mental Contrasting: Let's WOOP!	• Handout 6.5: Make It Stick!: Neuroplasticity	• Extending and Transferring the Concept

STUDENT ACTIVITIES
Neuroplasticity

Essential Question

- What factors influence your developing brain, and how can you use this information to grow as a thinker and problem solver?

Learning Objectives

By the end of this unit, I will . . .
- explore factors that influence the developing brain,
- demonstrate how information is transferred across neurons,
- study the works of key researchers who contributed to the understanding of neuroplasticity,
- practice mental contrasting, and
- develop a presentation connecting a researcher's work to my own life.

Name: _____ Date: _____

HANDOUT 6.1

Neuroplasticity

This handout previews many of the concepts that you will learn in this unit, including synapses, neuroplasticity, neurons, and growth mindset. This story started 50 years ago with a scientist and a snail . . .

Throughout the 1970s, Dr. Eric Kandel studied giant sea snails called aplysia. It wasn't that he was necessarily fascinated with snails. He was fascinated with the human brain and had a hunch that aplysia could help him understand how people learned. He chose this particular snail because it has a small number of rather large cells that are easy to see. He found that as aplysia learned, the **synapses**, or chemical structures between their cells changed. This was an exciting and important discovery, because previously many scientists believed that synapses, particularly those in the brain, developed to a certain point and were then unchanging.

Over the next several decades, Dr. Kandel demonstrated that all synapses, from those found in the marine snail to those in your teacher's brain, changed and adapted as a result of learning and experience. These changes are called **plasticity**, and when they occur in the brain, they are called **neuroplasticity**. In 2000, Dr. Kandel was awarded a Nobel Prize in Medicine for his work in helping people understand the power of neuroplasticity.

The brain is a continuously adapting work in progress. Our experiences play a powerful role in how it develops. When we wrestle with challenges, make new connections, or test a different approach, these are all powerful opportunities for our brains to learn. Looking at challenges as opportunities to learn is what researcher Dr. Carol Dweck called a **growth mindset**.

The brain seeks patterns and organizes those patterns through neural connections. When you learn something new, make new connections, retell an engaging lesson, or test an idea (even if it flops), you are helping to organize the neural pathways in your brain. The more your practice a skill or task, the faster your brain will follow that same pattern in the future. Think about how much effort it takes for a child to learn to read. You were once that child working to remember letter sounds, and now look at you! You can read poetry, novels, and fascinating articles on neuroscience.

In conclusion, our brains are not fixed. Instead they are constantly learning and adapting. The choices you make and experiences you have along the way can literally help rewire your brain.

References

Dweck, C. S. (2016). *Mindset: The new psychology of success*. Ballantine Books. (Original work published 2006)

The Nobel Prize. (n.d.). *Eric Kandel facts*. https://www.nobelprize.org/prizes/medicine/2000/kandel/facts

Neuroplasticity

HANDOUT 6.1, *continued*

Reading Comprehension and Thought Questions

1. Why was aplysia a good fit for Dr. Kandel's studies? _____

_____

_____

_____

2. In your own words, what was Dr. Kandel's big discovery? _____

_____

_____

_____

3. Looking at challenges as _____

_____

_____

_____ is an example of a growth mindset.

4. This text gave the example of a child learning to read. At one time in your life, you were just learning to read, and you are now able to read complicated texts. Give another example of something you worked really hard to learn.

_____

_____

_____

_____

5. Now give an example of something that is still hard for you but that you are working to learn.

_____

_____

_____

_____

Neuroplasticity

HANDOUT 6.2

Synapse Science

The human brain contains approximately 86 billion neurons. A **neuron** is a cell that sends information through electrical and chemical signals. In this activity, we will learn more about the anatomy of the neuron and act out **neurotransmission**, or the process through which information is shared across neurons.

Anatomy of a Neuron

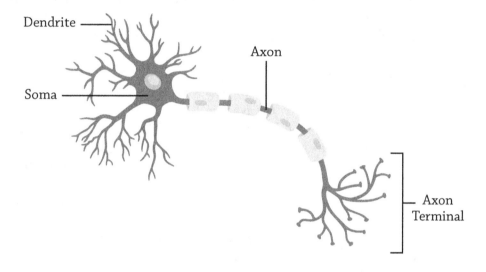

Neurotransmission: Act It Out

Let's act out the process of neurotransmission! First, review the following terms and definitions. Then, follow the acting directions to dramatize this process with a partner.

Term	Definition	Acting Directions
Synaptic cleft	The space/gap between neurons where messages/information are sent.	Make a very small bubble around you with your arms.
Dendrites	The branches of a neuron that deliver information to the cell.	Wiggle fingers excitedly.
Soma	The cell body containing the nucleus.	Stand in a superhero or power pose. Your body is the soma directing this message.

Neuroplasticity

HANDOUT 6.2, *continued*

Term	Definition	Acting Directions
Axon	A stem-like structure that takes information away from the cell and delivers it to the body.	Lock legs and stand up as tall as possible.
Axon Terminal	The end of a branch of a nerve's axon.	Wiggle toes, then flex as though you have just received an electrical current.

Working in pairs, face your partner. Double-check that you have left a **synaptic cleft** by making your arms into a bubble around you. One bubble is your neuron's space, and the other bubble is your partner's neuron's space. This space is very small—so small that your clothes touching another person could represent the dendrites. For our dramatization, we will exaggerate this space.

Select one person to send the message. This person is the presynaptic neuron (*presynaptic* means "before the synapse"). The other person will receive the message. This person is the postsynaptic neuron (*postsynaptic* means "after the synapse").

- The presynaptic neuron will send a message to the postsynaptic neuron through silent shouting. *Pretend as if you are screaming, yet no sound should escape your mouth.*
- The postsynaptic neuron will begin receiving the message through the **dendrites**. *Wiggle fingers excitedly.*
- Next the message will move to the **soma**, or cell body. *Stand in a superhero or power pose. Your body is the soma directing this message.*
- Then the message continues down the **axon**. *Lock legs and stand up as tall as possible.*
- Finally, the message reaches the **axon terminal**. *Wiggle toes, then flex and shake as though you have just received an electrical current.*

Once the message is received, switch roles.

HANDOUT 6.3
Growth Mindset Bingo

Carol Dweck, a researcher at Stanford University, studies success, failure, and the potential of neuroplasticity. Recognizing what neuroscientists have taught about how brains adapt based on experience and environment, Dr. Dweck teaches students to practice a **growth mindset** by welcoming challenges and embracing the possibility of "yet." Think of all of the great things you can achieve with great effort.

		Free Space		

Neuroplasticity

HANDOUT 6.3, *continued*

Directions: Choose 24 of these phrases/terms and populate your bingo card.

- I'm not great at that *yet*
- I love a challenge
- Neuroplasticity
- Synapse
- Let's learn from that
- Keep going
- Dendrite
- More effort = more learning
- Resilience
- Too easy = little learning
- Persistence
- Keep trying
- Mistakes matter, too
- This is tough, but so am I
- Soma

- Great approach
- Hard work matters
- Brains develop
- Neurons
- Malleable
- I'm testing an idea
- What are you working on?
- Axon
- Strategize
- Neurotransmission
- Synaptic cleft
- Carol Dweck
- Eric Kandel
- I think I can

Neuroplasticity

Growth Mindset Bingo Teacher Cards

The following are the bingo square phrases to cut out in advance of the lesson. You can fold these up and put them in a bowl or hat to draw from. This game offers lots of possibilities for extension.

I'm not great at that *yet*	I love a challenge	Neuroplasticity	Synapse	Let's learn from that
Keep going	Dendrite	More effort = more learning	Resilience	Too easy = little learning
Persistence	Keep trying	Mistakes matter, too	This is tough, but so am I	Soma
Great approach	Hard work matters	Brains develop	Neurons	Malleable
I'm testing an idea	What are you working on?	Axon	Strategize	Neuro-transmission
Synaptic cleft	Carol Dweck	Eric Kandel	I think I can	

Name: _____   Date: _____

Mental Contrasting: Let's WOOP!

Dr. Gabriele Oettingen is a motivational psychologist whose research shows how our wishes can serve as a first step toward achieving our dreams. However, these wishes must be followed with some strategic work. As part of the process, Dr. Oetingen asks us to contrast where we are right now with where we want to be and then use our problem-solving and planning skills to develop a pathway to get there. This is called **mental contrasting**. Let's try it!

W—WISH: Write down one specific wish you can reasonably work toward.

O—OUTCOME: What will it look like to achieve your wish? Have fun. Be specific.

O—OBSTACLE: What is standing in your way? Focus on things you can control.

P—PLAN: Write a plan for every obstacle you identified. Put your plans in action!

Note. Based on Oettingen et al.'s (2009) work on mental contrasting.

Brain-Based Learning With Gifted Students © Prufrock Press Inc.

Neuroplasticity

HANDOUT 6.5

Make It Stick!: Neuroplasticity

Challenge: Praxis Presentation

Praxis is when we apply research or theory to practice or behavior. In this unit, we learned about several researchers whose work has contributed to what we know about the brain's ability to persist through obstacles. Choose one of the researchers mentioned in the table and develop a presentation that addresses the following questions:

- Who was the researcher?
- What was their major discovery or contribution?
- Why does this matter in *your* life?
- How will you use this information to grow as a thinker and problem solver?

KEY TERMS

Neuron: A nerve cell that transmits information throughout the body.

Synaptic cleft: The space/gap between neurons where messages or information are sent.

Dendrites: The branches of a neuron that deliver information to the cell.

Soma: The cell body containing the nucleus.

Axon: A stem-like structure that takes information away from the cell and delivers it to the body.

Axon terminal: The end of a branch of a nerve's axon.

Neuroplasticity: The ability of the brain to reorganize (and grow) synaptic connections.

Growth mindset: A belief that with great effort we can learn and achieve great things.

Mental contrasting: A metacognitive model to connect our wishes and obstacles together to create meaningful plans.

Researcher	Concept
Dr. Eric Kandel	▪ Learning changes the chemical synapses of the brain. ▪ Through his first studies with a marine snail, Kandel demonstrated how memories and learning shape and even rewire the brain.
Dr. Carol Dweck	▪ Growth mindset. ▪ Her research shows that the ways we approach challenges and mistakes are essential to growth in learning.
Dr. Gabriele Oettingen	▪ Mental contrasting. ▪ Her research developed a metacognitive model called WOOP to help people develop plans to achieve their dreams.

Neuroplasticity

Extending and Transferring the Concept

This unit introduces students to basic concepts and theories surrounding neuroplasticity and neurotransmission. It also offers a high-level overview of how mindset and planning can help students persist through challenges. These concepts are ripe for classroom potential. The following are suggestions for possible extensions of the activities in this unit. Bring them to life in ways that make sense for your classroom community.

Handout 6.1: Neuroplasticity

- **KWL (Know/Want to Know/Learned):** The information in this handout lends itself to a KWL chart. Possible topics for this chart include: Neurons, Neuroplasticity, and Growth Mindset. Students can create a KWL in their lab books to work independently or develop classwide KWLs to refer to throughout the unit. Too often teachers miss some of the ongoing potential of KWL by using it only at the onset of a unit and at the very end. To get more leverage out of this practice, encourage students to continue generating questions (Want to Knows) throughout the unit. Some educators also add an S or R for "Still Want to Know" or "Research." As this unit concludes with a research project, the R may be a good fit here.

Handout 6.2: Synapse Science

- **Extend the drama:** The Act It Out activity gives students the opportunity to do a simple demonstration from one presynaptic neuron to one postsynaptic neuron. Challenge your class to extend the drama by involving more neurons and demonstrating a more complete message transfer. See the extension activity on neurotransmitters in Chapter 7 as a resource to help with this process.
- **Flip-book:** In addition to acting out the transfer of information across the synaptic cleft, challenge students to create a labeled flip-book that animates this process with sketches. These flip-books can be wonderful exit products for taking the lesson home to discuss with families.

Handout 6.3: Growth Mindset Bingo

See the Growth Mindset Bingo Teacher Cards for the phrases to prepare for the game. In order to get more leverage from this game, add definition and collaborative challenges, such as the following:

- **Define that:** Ask students to define the vocabulary words or give examples of when the various phrases could be used.
- **Make a skit:** Once a student earns a bingo, pause the game and ask small groups to create a skit using the winning bingo phrases. If the "free space" is one of the winning spaces, you can choose an outrageous word as a class (e.g., supercalifragilisticexpialidocious) to add humor and challenge to the skit.

Handout 6.4: Mental Contrasting: *Let's WOOP!*

- **Inside/outside my sphere of control:** An important aspect of mental contrasting is maximizing the things one can control. Before a person can do that, they have to recognize what is and isn't within their sphere of control. Play a sorting game with your students. Give each student a hula hoop, which represents their sphere of control. Students should stand in the center of their hula hoop. As you read the following wishes, if they are in the students' sphere of control, students may stay inside the circle. If they are not within the students' sphere of control, students must hop out of the circle.
  - Growing to 6 feet tall
  - Learning French
  - Traveling to China
  - Reading 100 books next year
  - Playing varsity soccer in high school
  - Building a greenhouse
  - Solving world hunger
  - Becoming president of the United States
  - Taking algebra in sixth grade
  - Becoming a veterinarian
  - Running a 6-minute mile
  - Learning how to fly a plane
  - Designing a new video game
  - Finding a cure for cancer
  - Making someone fall in love with you
  - Starting a new club at school

- Getting your little brother to be less annoying
- Winning $1,000,000 in the lottery
- Writing a book

Some of these statements are open for interpretation. Allow time for students to justify their decisions. This discussion about what they control, how they control it, and how they think about possibility is important. If students determine that a wish is outside their sphere of influence, ask how they could modify it to be within their control. Ask students how their sphere of control shifts if they set a timeline on the wishes (e.g., by the end of this school year).

Handout 6.5: **Make It Stick!:** *Neuroplasticity*

- **Showcase:** These presentations again lend themselves to a showcase event. Students can practice presentation and graphic design skills using Google Slides, PowerPoint, Prezi, or VoiceThread to create polished presentations to present to families or others in your learning communities.

Additional Extensions

The following are even more ideas to help transfer these lessons on neuroplasticity beyond the activities in this unit.

- **Growth mindset cards:** In Chapter 3, students learned about the power of thinking self-talk. In this unit, they learned about growth mindset and how their approach to challenges can affect the likelihood of overcoming those challenges and learning. Building off the growth mindset bingo terms, have students create a classroom set of growth mindset encouragement (or reminder) cards. You can give these cards to students as encouraging reminders, or students can give these cards to their peers when needed. The intention with this practice is to create a supportive classroom culture that values process and persistence.
- **Environment studies:** Although the activities in this unit introduce the idea that the environment affects brain development, they don't expand on how or what a healthy or unhealthy environment might look like.
  - Ask students to design growth mindset classrooms. What would these classrooms look, sound, and feel like?

- As a class, study the effects of stress and boredom on the brain and problem solve how to handle stress in healthy ways. (See Chapter 7 for some ideas.)
- Dig deeper into the science behind neurogenesis and epigenetics to learn about how genes and neurons change and adapt according to environmental factors. If possible, invite a guest expert to visit your classroom and explore these concepts with students.

Emotional Regulation

ESSENTIAL QUESTIONS

- How are your emotions, behaviors, and thoughts connected?
- What does this connection look like in the brain?

BIG IDEAS IN SCIENCE

- Structure and Function
- Interdependence

Validating and Regulating Emotions in the Classroom

Every day, students experience a range of emotions. These emotions have a powerful influence on the classroom. How students feel directly affects how they learn. Likewise, how teachers feel directly affects how they teach (Martin & Ochsner, 2016). Although there are patterns across people's emotional responses, emotions are also highly individualized and directly influenced by unique experiences, memories, and personalities. In biological terms, emotions are the brain's response to stimuli or experiences. Life presents students with a diverse array of stimuli, from the challenges of tackling algebra ahead of their peers, to winning a science competition, to connecting (or not connecting) with a friend group, to finding that book or song that speaks directly to their soul. The brain, particularly the complex system of nerves and networks known as *the limbic system*, helps students respond to, process, and make sense of these stimuli.

Although some are certainly more pleasant than others, there are no "good" or "bad" emotions. Instead, emotions are information. *Emotional regulation* helps students (and teachers) better understand and respond to their complex feelings. As people get older, they tend to become more adept at emotional regulation. One gifted student described it to me in this way: "It's learning strategies to give me some control over my emotions rather than always feeling like my emotions are controlling me."

KEY CONCEPT

Emotional regulation: The process by which one recognizes, experiences, and responds to feelings.

- **Explicit emotional regulation:** A conscious effort to use strategies to respond to emotions.

- **Implicit emotional regulation:** Automatic processes in response to emotions.

Emotions interact and influence each other (Okon-Singer et al., 2015). For example, when a person is deeply angry, they are less likely to experience joy. However, by recognizing, naming, and processing that anger, they may be able to both regulate it and create space for additional emotions such as joy. Likewise, when a person is persisting toward a goal, sometimes their feelings of pride or joy are enhanced by earlier experiences with frustration or sadness that occurred as they strove for this goal. Teachers can help students with strategies to improve their explicit emotional regulation skills. This starts with five basic premises shown in Figure 12.

When it comes to emotion, neuroscience supports what teachers have long suspected: How students feel affects how they learn. Emotion and cognition are not separate processes. Instead, the complex interplay of emotional processing and cognitive processing reveals a coordinated response across brain structures with consequences for attention, working memory, and executive functioning (Okon-Singer et al., 2015). Neuroscientists are continuing to learn more about how and where emotion happens in the brain.

The Neuroanatomy of Emotions: A Look at the Limbic System

This unit focuses on key structures of the limbic system. Although this is not a comprehensive overview of all brain structures involved in emotional processing, it is a good starting place as teachers and students build a working knowledge of the neuroscience of emotional regulation. To extend your study on the neuroanatomy of emotions, see the extension resources.

The *limbic system* is a set of brain structures that play a significant role in the formation of memories, emotional processing, and behaviors. Use the mnemonic *Hippos' Teeth Have Awful Odor* to help students remember the major parts of the limbic system: hippocampus, thalamus, hypothalamus, amygdala, and olfactory bulb (see Figure 13):

- **Hippocampus:** Shaped like a curved tube or a seahorse, this structure stores visual-spatial and verbal memories. This area is susceptible to damage by long-term stress and impacted early in Alzheimer's disease.
- **Thalamus:** Receives and filters sensory information or sensations that can be interpreted as pain, touch, temperature, etc. Almost all sensory information is relayed to the thalamus, making it essential for perception.
- **Hypothalamus:** As the name suggests, this structure is located under the thalamus. It links the endocrine and nervous systems. Through neurohormone secretion, this structure is responsible for drives such as thirst, hunger, or readying for attack. In late elementary and early middle school, it also plays an important role in puberty by producing the *gonadotropin releasing hormone* (GnRH).
- **Amygdala:** Almond-shaped structure that responds to fear, hormones, and memory. The amygdala enhances emotional memories encoded in

FIGURE 12
Emotional Regulation in the Classroom

EMOTIONS ARE INFORMATION

There aren't good or bad emotions. That said, people can make better choices in responding to emotions, and they can improve at choosing these strategies.

FEELINGS ARE VALID

The same situation may lead to different emotions for different people. Everyone has the right to name their own emotions. The way students say they are feeling is valid.

EMOTIONS CAN INFLUENCE BEHAVIOR AND ATTENTION

It's hard for students to think clearly when a big emotion is using up so much brain power.

EMOTION-BEHAVIOR CONNECTION CAN HELP

Students and teachers can use specific strategies to respond to emotional information. These different strategies work differently for everyone, as each person is a unique processor.

LEARNING ABOUT EMOTIONS MATTERS

The more students know about emotions and how emotional processing works, the better able they are to respond to complex feelings.

the hippocampus. When alerted to a possible threat, the amygdala sends a stress signal or alarm across the brain, particularly to the hypothalamus.

- **Olfactory bulb:** *Olfaction* is the scientific term for sense of smell. Olfaction begins when a fragrance enters the nasal cavity. The olfactory bulb sends sensory signals that do not go through the thalamus. It processes these fragrances and connects them to other information in the brain. Due, in part, to direct connections with the amygdala and the hippocampus, smells often trigger a strong and immediate emotional connection.

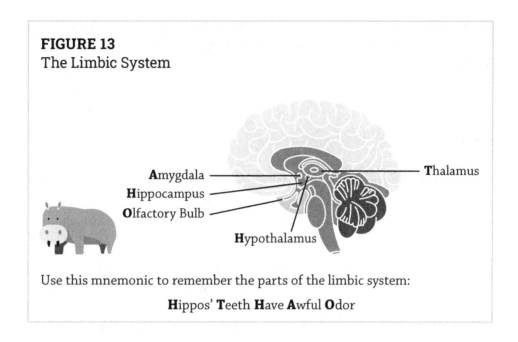

FIGURE 13
The Limbic System

Amygdala

Hippocampus

Olfactory Bulb

Hypothalamus

Thalamus

Use this mnemonic to remember the parts of the limbic system:

Hippos' **T**eeth **H**ave **A**wful **O**dor

Emotional Regulation in the Gifted Classroom

Supportive, affirming environments are best at fostering learning and development for all students, including gifted children. The intense emotional needs of gifted youth have been well studied by scholars in gifted education (see Hoge & Renzulli, 1993; Kerr, 1994; Kerr & Foley Nipcon, 2003; Kerr & McKay, 2014; Lovecky, 2011; Rimm, 1999). The cause of this emotional intensity is the subject of some debate. Likely, neurobiological differences between gifted youth and the general population, as well as environmental factors such as limited services for and understanding of gifted youth, contribute to this intensity. Responding to the intense emotions of gifted students often requires specialized understanding and care (Fiedler, 1999; Lovecky, 1994; Robbins, 2006).

Classroom emotions are often "contagious." For example, if you are feeling anxious while leading a lesson, sometimes the whole class becomes anxious in response. Likewise, an angry outburst can change the emotional temperature of the entire class. Recognizing the important interplay of emotions allows teachers to guard against reflecting negative emotions when they appear in our classroom. For instance, to help students regulate, teachers should not match anger with anger. Instead, they can strive to match anger with calm affirmation. By affirming students' emotional experiences as valid, asking children to name their own emotions, and helping them talk through what triggered the feeling and how they want to respond, teachers can often deescalate a volatile situation, teach emotional regulation, and contribute to a calmer classroom environment. As a class community, everyone from teachers to students can practice recognizing, naming, and regulating their emotions, particularly those that interfere with learning or *prosocial behaviors*.

KEY CONCEPT

Prosocial behaviors: Helping behaviors; those actions that are motivated by a concern for the feelings and welfare of others. For example, acting out of empathy is a prosocial behavior.

Emotional regulation and prosocial behaviors are teachable skills. However, outside of early elementary classrooms often these affective skills are not explicitly included in curriculum and instruction. Research shows that when teachers directly teach prosocial behaviors and emotional regulation strategies, students see marked improvement across these areas (Flook et al., 2015). Given the asynchronous development of gifted students who often present with emotional intensity, these skills and strategies are essential in gifted programming (see particularly the NAGC [2019] programming standards for Learning and Development and Learning Environments).

Teaching about emotional regulation and reframing how students think about emotions can be an empowering topic of inquiry in the classroom. The *cognitive triangle* refers to the ways that feelings, thoughts, and behaviors are connected. By recognizing the connection between feeling, thinking, and doing, teachers can help students recognize emotions as information and make choices about how they want to use or respond to their big feelings of joy, anger, grief, pride, worry, and frustration. This puts students in the driver's seat of their thinking, behaviors, and feelings in ways they may not have experienced previously.

KEY CONCEPT

Learning domains: Educational psychologists reference three primary learning domains: cognitive domain (thinking), affective domain (feeling), and a psychomotor domain (doing). These domains are deeply interconnected.

Understanding emotional regulation and the important link between feeling and learning is essential for effective lesson planning and instruction. Although all three learning domains inform how teachers write lesson plans and curriculum, starting with the affective domain helps prime the brain for learning and development (see Figure 14). The affective domain includes feelings, emotions, motivations, and personal and social development (Ferguson, 2006; Gilligan, 1982; Gilligan et al., 1988; Hoge & Renzulli, 1993; NAGC, n.d.-b). Affective education explores the "tenuous, albeit symbiotic, relationship between social-emotional and cognitive needs" (Fishman-Weaver, 2018, p. 34). If left unaddressed, these social-emotional needs can lead to the *masked affective crisis* (Fishman-Weaver, 2018), which is of particular concern for gifted and high-achieving students.

KEY CONCEPT

Masked affective crisis: This term refers to the ways that academic achievement can overshadow the social-emotional needs of academically high-achieving youth, particularly gifted young women. As a result, counselors and teachers sometimes miss or respond retroactively to social-emotional issues long after intervention is needed. This concept emerged from my longitudinal study (2009–2015) with gifted youth (see *Wholehearted Teaching of Gifted Young Women*; Fishman-Weaver, 2018).

KEY TERMS FOR EDUCATORS

- **Cognitive triangle:** How thoughts, emotions and behaviors are interconnected and dependent; focusing on one can have an impact across all three.
- **Emotional regulation:** The process by which a person recognizes, experiences, and responds to feelings.
- **Limbic system:** A set of brain structures that play a significant role in the formation of memories, emotional processing, and behaviors.
- **Olfaction:** Scientific term for sense of smell.

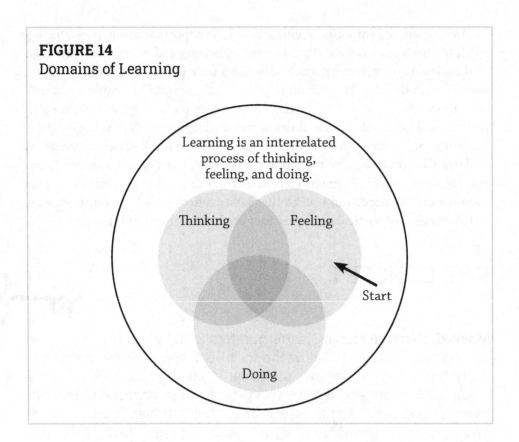

FIGURE 14
Domains of Learning

Learning is an interrelated process of thinking, feeling, and doing.

Thinking

Feeling

Start

Doing

Classroom Application

Unit Overview

In this unit, students learn specific strategies to practice emotional regulation. The springboard text introduces the Stop-Name-React method for responding to big feelings. Next, students work on developing their emotional vocabulary and emotional literacy. This activity builds on the six basic emotions that psychologist Paul Ekman identified in the 1970s (Ekman, 1992). Ekman's later work and subsequent psychologists building off of his studies have suggested that there may be more than six basic emotions and also that people experience a unique combinations of these emotions. Next, students practice a mindfulness breathing exercise drawing on the work of Buddhist monk Thích Nhất Hạnh (2015). Continuing with neuroanatomical studies, the last activity in this unit is an overview of the limbic system.

Key takeaways for students (and teachers) include that emotions offer valid information; that one's thoughts, feelings, and behaviors are interconnected; and that there are specific strategies one can use to become more adept at emotional regulation. The "make it stick" challenge for this unit synthesizes these takeaways by asking students to be independent investigators in their own emotions and responses through collecting data for one week. After one week of data collection, students complete an analysis summary on what they have learned and what they would like to focus on next.

Time Suggestions

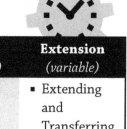

Class 1 (20 minutes)	Class 2 (25 minutes)	Class 3 (30 minutes)	Class 4 (30 minutes)	Extension (variable)
▪ Handout 7.1: What Can I Do With This Feeling? ▪ Essential Questions and Learning Objectives	▪ Handout 7.2: Building an Emotional Vocabulary	▪ Handout 7.3: Mindful Breathing ▪ Handout 7.4: A Look at the Limbic System	▪ Handout 7.5: Make It Stick!: Emotional Regulation	▪ Extending and Transferring the Concept

Name: _____ Date: _____

STUDENT ACTIVITIES
Emotional Regulation

Essential Questions

- How are your emotions, behaviors, and thoughts connected?
- What does this connection look like in the brain?

Learning Objectives

By the end of this unit, I will . . .
- explain the ways thoughts, feelings, and behaviors are connected;
- build my emotional vocabulary;
- practice strategies to cultivate mindfulness;
- label and explain the key structures of the limbic system; and
- conduct a weeklong investigation of emotions and emotional regulation strategies.

Brain-Based Learning With Gifted Students © Prufrock Press Inc.

Emotional Regulation

Name: _____ Date: _____

HANDOUT 7.1

What Can I Do With This Feeling?

Do you feel like you control your emotions, or do you feel like your emotions control you? Maybe it's a little bit of both?

In biological terms, emotions are our brains' response to experiences. Life is chock-full of many different experiences, from celebrating a birthday, to tackling a difficult assignment, to processing the passing of a grandparent; from seeing a gorgeous sunset, to coming across a dead frog; from coming home to someone making cookies, to getting over the flu. Our brains—particularly the complex system of nerves and networks known as **the limbic system**—help us respond to, process, and make sense of these stimuli.

Sometimes it might seem like your emotions are controlling you. There you are, going about your schoolwork, and then bam—your teacher says something, you get to a certain part of the assignment, your friend does something, or you think of something that happened last summer—all of a sudden you are feeling a big emotion, like anger, frustration, anxiety, panic, stress, or sadness, and you might not even be sure why. You're no longer concentrating on your schoolwork; you're just dealing with this big feeling and hoping others don't notice as it grows and grows and grows.

I have some good news for you. First, that feeling is 100% normal. We've all been there. Second, there are some strategies you can learn to take some control over your emotions. These strategies are called **emotional regulation**.

Do you remember what to do if you catch on fire? Stop, drop, and roll. If a big emotion catches you by surprise, you can take a similar approach: Stop-Name-React.

- **Stop:** First, you have to pause. If you're working on a math problem, stop multiplying for a moment.
- **Name:** Next, name your feeling. When you name your sadness as sadness or your exacerbation (another word for "extreme frustration") as exacerbation, these emotions have a little less control over you.
- **React:** Finally, decide what you are going to do with that feeling. How are you going to respond? Are you going to go get a drink of water? Are you going to take a deep breath? Are you going to talk to your teacher? Are you going to ask to call a family member? Are you going to squeeze your hand into a tight fist and then release? Are you going to practice some positive self-talk? When you choose how you are going to respond, you put yourself back in control.

STOP
Pause for a moment.

NAME
Identify your feeling.

REACT
Choose an action.

This doesn't mean that the emotion goes away or that it should. Emotions are information that help us understand and experience life. Part of being human and navigating life is experiencing a huge range of emotions. Each human being is unique. A different way to think about this is that nobody is better at being you than you.

HANDOUT 7.1, *continued*

Comprehension and Reflection Questions

1. Do you feel like you control your emotions, or do you feel like your emotions control you? Defend your answer.

   _____

   _____

   _____

   _____

2. What are some of your most memorable experiences? Did your emotions define them?

   _____

   _____

   _____

3. What are the three steps to take when a big emotion catches you by surprise? Imagine that all of a sudden you were overwhelmed with frustration. How could you use these steps to approach this big feeling?

   _____

   _____

   _____

4. The author writes, "Emotions are information that help us understand and experience life." What does this mean? How can emotions, even the tough ones, help you experience life?

   _____

   _____

   _____

   _____

Emotional Regulation

HANDOUT 7.2

Building an Emotional Vocabulary

In this activity, we will develop our emotional vocabulary and our emotional literacy. **Emotional vocabulary** includes all of the words you know to describe feelings. According to Dr. Lorea Martinez (2017), there are 3,000 words in the English language to describe emotions, but most people use less than 20 on a regular basis. **Emotional literacy** is being able to express your own emotions and identify emotional cues from others.

The following chart will help you name and describe different emotions to enhance your emotional literacy.

Emotions	What are some synonyms? *Challenge yourself to think of examples before looking any up.*	What does it look like? *What visual cues can you see when someone is having this feeling?*	What does it sound like? *What might someone say or exclaim when having this feeling?*	How can this emotion help you? *What are good things that might happen from having this feeling?*
Happiness				
Sadness				
Disgust				

Name: _____ Date: _____

Emotions	What are some synonyms? *Challenge yourself to think of examples before looking any up.*	What does it look like? *What visual cues can you see when someone is having this feeling?*	What does it sound like? *What might someone say or exclaim when having this feeling?*	How can this emotion help you? *What are good things that might happen from having this feeling?*
Fear				
Surprise				
Anger				

Reference

Martinez, L. (2017). *Got SEL? Teaching students to describe emotions.* Edutopia. https://www.edutopia.org/discussion/got-sel-teaching-students-describe-emotions

HANDOUT 7.3
Mindful Breathing

In, out
Deep, slow
Calm, ease
Smile, release
Present moment,
wonderful moment.

Practicing mindfulness starts with the breath. Find a place in the room where you feel comfortable. Either sit cross-legged or lie down on your back. Place your hand on your stomach, so you can feel your breath filling your diaphragm. *Close your eyes softly and notice your breath.* It may take a few moments to calm down enough to really notice your breath as you inhale and exhale. Once the room quiets, your teacher will read to you a short breathing meditation (shown on the right) by the Buddhist monk Thích Nhất Hạnh. With each word, breathe in or out. Your teacher will read these lines several times to help your breathing adjust to the meditation. Try to focus only on your breath. If your mind wanders, simply notice that it is wandering and bring your attention back to your breathing.

Reference

Hanh, T. N. (2015). *The heart of the Buddha's teaching: Transforming suffering into peace, joy, and liberation*. Harmony. (Original work published 1999)

Comprehension and Reflection Questions

1. We are always breathing. Most of the time, how aware are you of your breath? Why do you think that is?

   _____

   _____

   _____

2. How did you feel before this exercise? How did you feel afterward?

   _____

   _____

   _____

3. What can this practice teach you about the connection between your thoughts, feelings, and behaviors?

   _____

   _____

   _____

Emotional Regulation

HANDOUT 7.4

A Look at the Limbic System

The **limbic system** is a set of brain structures that play a significant role in the formation of memories, emotional processing, and behaviors. You can use the mnemonic **Hippos' Teeth Have Awful Odor** to help you remember the major parts of the limbic system: hippocampus, thalamus, hypothalamus, amygdala, and olfactory bulb.

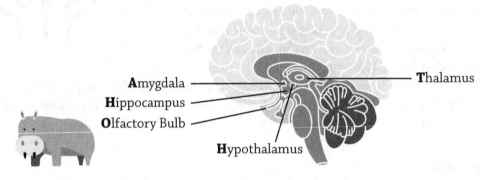

Use this mnemonic to remember the parts of the limbic system:

Hippos' **T**eeth **H**ave **A**wful **O**dor

- **Hippocampus:** The hippocampus is a structure shaped like a curved tube or seahorse that stores visual-spatial and verbal memories. This area is susceptible to damage by long-term stress and impacted early in Alzheimer's disease. The mnemonic helps you with the first part of this structure's name, *hippo*. You can remember the second part of the word, *campus*, by thinking of this structure as the memory campus of the brain.
- **Thalamus:** The thalamus receives and filters sensory information or sensations that can be interpreted as pain, touch, temperature, etc. Almost all sensory information is relayed to the thalamus, making it essential for perception, or that feeling when you just know something.
- **Hypothalamus:** The prefix *hypo* means "under," and so, as you might guess, the hypothalamus is located under the thalamus. It is responsible for drives such as thirst, hunger, or readying for attack.
- **Amygdala:** This almond-shaped structure responds to fear, hormones, and memory. When alerted to a possible threat, the amygdala sends a stress signal or alarm across the brain, particularly to the hypothalamus.
- **Olfactory bulb:** What might an old factory smell like? Think about it for a second. This may seem like a weird question, but it might just help you remember this structure in the limbic system. *Olfaction* is the scientific term for sense of smell. Olfaction begins when a fragrance enters the nasal cavity. The olfactory bulb processes these fragrances and connects them to other information in the brain. Smells often have a strong connection to feelings and memories, partially due to the fact that the olfactory bulb is closely connected with the amygdala and the hippocampus. In the mnemonic, the "O" word is *odor*, which might also help you remember the function of this structure.

Name: _____ Date: _____

Make It Stick!: Emotional Regulation

In this unit, we learned that emotions give us important information; that our thoughts, feelings, and behaviors are interconnected; and that there are strategies we can use to become more effective at emotional regulation.

Key Concepts: Emotional Regulation

Concept	Notes
What can I do with a big feeling?	**Stop-Name-React:** This emotional regulation strategy helps give you more control over big emotions when they come.
Emotional regulation	As you get older, your brain develops some automatic responses that help you regulate your feelings. However, there are also intentional strategies you can learn to manage and process your emotions. Like all skills, you can improve these through practice.
Emotional vocabulary and emotional literacy	These terms refer to the ability to talk about and recognize your own emotions as well as the emotional cues of others.
Mindfulness	Mindfulness is the practice of being aware of the present moment, including noticing your breath, feelings, thoughts, and how your body is responding. Practicing mindfulness often leads to greater awareness and calm.
The limbic system	A set of brain structures that play a significant role in the formation of memories, emotional processing, and behaviors. Test yourself to see if you can remember the major structures of the limbic system using the mnemonic *Hippos' Teeth Have Awful Odor*.

Challenge: Emotional Regulation, An Independent Investigation

Over the next week, practice some of the emotional regulation strategies you've learned in this unit such as:
- stop, name, react;
- mindful breathing; and
- responding to others' emotional cues.

Along the way, record data on your feelings and any strategies you use to respond to these feelings.

Emotional Regulation

HANDOUT 7.5, *continued*

The lab sheet includes one more research-based practice to try this week—gratitude. At the end of every day, either after dinner or just before bedtime, take a moment to reflect on your day and write down three reasons you have to be thankful. All of these strategies take practice. Just do your best!

After 5 days of data tracking, complete the analysis summary.

Lab Sheet

	Morning	Afternoon	Evening
Day 1 Date: _____ Three reasons to be thankful today:	Key emotions: What events might have caused these feelings: How I responded:	Key emotions: What events might have caused these feelings: How I responded:	Key emotions: What events might have caused these feelings: How I responded:

Name: _____ Date: _____

	Morning	Afternoon	Evening
Day 2 Date: _____ Three reasons to be thankful today:	Key emotions: What events might have caused these feelings: How I responded:	Key emotions: What events might have caused these feelings: How I responded:	Key emotions: What events might have caused these feelings: How I responded:
Day 3 Date: _____ Three reasons to be thankful today:	Key emotions: What events might have caused these feelings: How I responded:	Key emotions: What events might have caused these feelings: How I responded:	Key emotions: What events might have caused these feelings: How I responded:

Emotional Regulation

Name: _____ Date: _____

	Morning	Afternoon	Evening
Day 4 Date: _____ Three reasons to be thankful today:	Key emotions: What events might have caused these feelings: How I responded:	Key emotions: What events might have caused these feelings: How I responded:	Key emotions: What events might have caused these feelings: How I responded:
Day 5 Date: _____ Three reasons to be thankful today:	Key emotions: What events might have caused these feelings: How I responded:	Key emotions: What events might have caused these feelings: How I responded:	Key emotions: What events might have caused these feelings: How I responded:

Emotional Regulation

Name: _____ Date: _____

HANDOUT 7.5, *continued*

Analysis Summary

1. What patterns do you notice in looking at your data? _____
   _____
   _____
   _____

2. What surprised you in completing this investigation? _____
   _____
   _____
   _____

3. Which emotional regulation strategies were easiest for you to apply, and which were the most difficult?
   _____
   _____
   _____
   _____

4. What does this project teach you about the relationship between your thoughts, feelings, and behaviors?
   _____
   _____
   _____
   _____

5. Based on your data and analysis, set one goal you would like to implement next week.
   _____
   _____
   _____
   _____

Extending and Transferring the Concept

This unit introduces students to basic concepts surrounding emotional regulation, including emotional vocabulary, emotional literacy, mindful breathing, and gratitude. Most of these strategies center around the cognitive triangle. In addition to learning about the psychology of emotional regulation, students also continue with their neuroanatomical studies by exploring the limbic system. All of these activities have endless potential for extension. The following are a few suggestions for ways you might deepen learning around these concepts in your classroom.

Handout 7.1: What Can I Do With This Feeling?

- **Act it out:** Give students safe opportunities to practice Stop-Name-React by acting out scenarios in small groups. As a class, create a list of settings (classroom, playground, cafeteria, school hallway, kitchen, school bus, etc.) and a list of big emotions (happiness, disgust, anger, sadness, shock, etc.). Create one jar of settings and another of emotions. Working in groups of 3–4, have students select a setting and an emotion. They will then have 10 minutes to organize a short skit in which a character uses Stop-Name-React to respond to their chosen emotion. Groups should perform their skits for the class. After each skit, talk through what you notice, how the character used Stop-Name-React, and other possibilities the character might have chosen.

Handout 7.2: Building an Emotional Vocabulary

- **Emotional literacy charades:** Once students have brainstormed synonyms for the six basic emotions, create an emotional vocabulary word wall. You can then use this emotional vocabulary word wall to help students build emotional literacy through charades. In this game, a student chooses one of the terms on the word wall and does their best to act it out to the class. Students then have to guess what emotion is being performed. This activity helps students attend to the nonverbals and nuances among different emotions.

Handout 7.3: Mindful Breathing

- **Mindful tasting:** Another great way to introduce students to the concept of mindfulness, or being aware of the present moment, is through mindful tasting. Citrus fruits and chocolates are especially good for an introduction to this idea.
    - First give students a small piece of chocolate or piece of a citrus fruit and ask them to eat it as they normally would.
    - Next give students another piece of chocolate or citrus fruit and explain that they are going to eat this one mindfully. This means drawing all of their awareness to the task at hand. Before they eat the snack, they might look at it for a moment, noticing any irregularities or characteristics. They might smell the snack, thereby cuing their olfactory bulb. When they do eat the snack, they should do so mindfully, noticing the flavors and the ways the flavors change as they continue to enjoy this treat (e.g., the chocolate melting slowly, the citrus fizzing).
    - Afterward, ask students how this second experience was different from the first, how it relates to the work they did on mindful breathing, and what it might teach them about the power of awareness.

Handout 7.4: A Look at the Limbic System

- **Neuroanatomical trading cards:** Extend your neuroanatomical learning by studying key neurotransmitters associated with emotions and emotional regulation. See the examples in Figure 15. You can extend this idea further by having students create their own cards with information from previous lessons on neuroanatomy. For example, what would the amygdala card have on it? What would its nickname and key statistics or qualities be?

Handout 7.5: Make It Stick!: *Emotional Regulation*

- **Movie celebration:** Disney Pixar's *Inside Out* (Docter, 2015) does a wonderful job of illustrating many of the concepts in this unit in a student-friendly way. While watching the film, ask students to keep track of how the basic emotions are displayed, what information these emotions give the main character, what emotional regulation strategies the protagonist or other characters learn during the film, and how the different structures of the limbic system are represented.

165

FIGURE 15
Neuroanatomical Trading Cards: Neurotransmitters

The Feel-Good Fan Dopamine

Dopamine causes us to want, to seek out, and to search. It is linked to the brain's reward/pleasure system. Dopamine contributes to the joy we experience in a delicious piece of cake or the excited focus rush we get when working with flow on an interesting project. It fuels curiosity.

Too much of a good thing?
Dopamine is also linked to addiction and dangerous levels of sensation seeking.

The Fight or Flight Bodybuilder Norepinephrine (NE)

Sometimes called the stress hormone, NE helps us prepare for fight or flight.

- **Fight:** Before a big exam, NE can help increase the amount of oxygen to your brain to allow you to think more clearly.
- **Flight:** NE can also increase your heart rate to allow more blood to rush to your muscles if you need to run away from danger.

Excessive NE can be related to test anxiety.

A Well-Being Wonder Serotonin

This neurotransmitter affects several brain-body functions and connections, from digestion and eating behaviors to sleep/wakefulness and mood. Serotonin helps regulate the gastrointestinal tract, including when we are full/satisfied, hungry, or nauseated. Getting enough light, exercising, and eating nutritious foods are natural ways to increase serotonin.

Not enough of a good thing? Low levels of serotonin have been linked to depression.

The Regulators GABA and Glutamate

GABA and glutamate are the brain's most plentiful neurotransmitters. They help regulate the flow and intensity of neurotransmission.

- GABA is an *inhibitory postsynaptic potential*. This means it decreases the likelihood that the neuron will fire an action potential. GABA helps us stay calm, think clearly, rest, and avoid getting overwhelmed.
- Glutamate is an *excitatory postsynaptic potential*. This means it increases the likelihood that the neuron will fire an action potential. Glutamate helps prime the body and brain for focus, learning, and memory.

Additional Extensions

The following are some suggestions to transfer these concepts beyond this unit and apply them to create a more cohesive schoolwide culture.

- **Analyzing amygdala triggers:** Help students use neuroanatomical language, including *amygdala triggers* and *activate my prefrontal cortex*. Figure 16 is a thought sheet students can use to begin thinking about how stress and fear present in their bodies.

KEY CONCEPT

Amygdala trigger: When the amygdala senses stress or danger it elicits a *stress response*. Sometimes the response is rapid, such as when jumping out of the way of oncoming traffic. Sometimes the response builds, such as when encountering an angry friend or stepping onto a stage to give a speech. In those less immediate situations, individuals often experience physical signs that a stress response has been activated. These may include tightening of the throat or chest, sweaty palms, clenched jaw or fists. The way fear and stress present in the body is different for every person, so teachers should guide students in identifying their own amygdala triggers. In this way, teachers can show students how to counter their amygdala trigger with a calm response and/or with an intention to activate the prefrontal cortex (see Chapter 4).

- **Share your learning:** Getting school faculty on the same page about nurturing emotional regulation can help students practice these skills across classes and grades. Use this chapter to offer an in-house professional development on emotional regulation. You might share some of the readings from this chapter as well as the activities on analyzing amygdala triggers or activating the prefrontal cortex (see Chapter 4, Figure 8). Your students can also create PSA posters on these concepts to decorate the school hallways. The more consistent strategies teachers can use across classrooms, the more cohesive the school culture will be around helping children process and respond to big emotions in healthy and effective ways.

FIGURE 16
Amygdala Triggers Thought Sheet

Name:

AMYGDALA TRIGGERS

When the amygdala senses stress or danger, it signals a stress response. We often experience physical signs when a stress response has been activated. With practice, sometimes we can respond to these triggers with calm and reason. First, however, we have to learn what stress or fear feels like for us.

What does stress or fear feel like in your body?

I Feel: _____

I Feel: _____

I Feel: _____

It is normal, and even healthy, to occasionally experience stress or fear. Although you can develop strategies to respond differently to some stressors, it is important to talk with a trusted adult if you ever feel unsafe.

Chapter 8

Keeping the Brain Healthy

ESSENTIAL QUESTIONS

- What choices can you make to take better care of your brain?
- How can you be an advocate for brain health?

BIG IDEAS IN SCIENCE

- Structure and Function
- Interdependence

Cultivating Brain Health in the Classroom

Children learn best in environments where they have access to the basic resources needed for growth and development and where they are supported, challenged, and safe. Access to basic resources, including nutrition, healthcare, mental healthcare, and clean water, has an impact on students' physical health, including their brain development and mental acuity. Knowing that children do not have equitable access to healthcare and healthy environments, a chapter on cultivating brain health in the classroom would be incomplete without also including a discussion on (1) the imperative roles public schools play in protecting the public health of school children and (2) the stark social inequalities that exist in the U.S. and abroad. In many ways, cultivating brain health requires the same health practices as taking care of general health, including eating a well-balanced diet, getting enough sleep, limiting harmful stress, staying hydrated, and having access to safe, engaging learning environments. Although public school teachers do imperative work to safeguard all of these health practices, children continue to have unequal access to them.

According to the United States Department of Agriculture (USDA, 2019), 6 million children in the U.S. lived in food-insecure households in 2018. The American Academy of Pediatrics and the Food Research and Action Center (2017) reported that "food insecurity—even marginal food insecurity—is detrimental to children's health and well-being. For example, food insecurity can lead to poor health status, developmental risk, mental health problems, and poor educational outcomes" (p. 7). Schools engage in critical work to mitigate food insecurity through the school lunch, breakfast, and afterschool and snack programs, which provide free or reduced-cost meals to qualifying families. In 2018, the school lunch program, the largest USDA-funded food program for children, provided low-cost or free lunches to 29.7 million children daily (USDA, 2019). Better understanding the role these essential resources have on the health and learning outcomes of children will lead communities and policy leaders to purposefully address access gaps and to conceptualize school as a public health initiative.

As you consider the conditions to cultivating brain health in the classroom, remember that the interplay of multiple variables holds the greatest effect on overall well-being. For example, "Considerable evidence links physical activity and optimal energy intake with improved mood and cognitive function" (Dauncey, 2012, p. 583). Health is holistic and multivariable. Children learn best in environments where they have access to the basic resources (including nutrition) needed for growth and development and where they are supported, challenged, and safe.

KEY CONCEPT

Brain health: An umbrella term for mental, physical, and social cognitive well-being. Key factors of quality brain health include nutrition, hydration, sleep, exercise/fitness, supportive and challenging learning environments, and feelings of belonging/connectedness.

Nutrition

Nutrition is essential for healthy brain development. Like all factors outlined in this chapter, nutrition must be considered within a multivariable context. Adequate balanced nutrition has important positive effects on overall health, including brain development and function. The foods and nutrients a child consumes affect the structure and function of their brain, including their ability to learn and concentrate. Although nutrition matters throughout a person's lifetime, there are critical periods in childhood (and also during prenatal care) when access to specific nutrients directly affects brain development. For example, birth to 2 years, 7 to 9 years, and the mid-teenage years are all sensitive or critical windows for frontal lobe development. Adequate nutrition (or lack of nutrition) during these times may have an even more profound effect on frontal lobe development and function than during other periods (Bryan et al., 2004). Figure 17 outlines the role of macronutrients in the typical diet.

Of the three macronutrients, proteins tend to be the most expensive (meaning least accessible) and also the ones I most frequently need to encourage my students to eat more of. Therefore, I want to spend a moment highlighting the dangers of protein energy malnutrition (PEM) or protein deficiencies. Results from PEM studies show that PEM in infancy and early childhood can have lasting effects on IQ scores and school performance into the teen years (Bryan et al., 2004). As PEM is not a single variable, children (and adults) with PEM often also present with other nutrient deficiencies (Fuglestad et al., 2008).

Making sure that children eat and have access to a protein-rich diet, particularly at breakfast and lunch, is important for their overall health and brain development. Teachers can help students understand the important role protein plays in creating enzymes, hormones, antibodies, and neurotransmitters, and in helping the body build and repair tissue. Teachers can also point out protein options in school breakfasts and lunch, and model sound nutritional habits, including getting enough lean protein.

FIGURE 17
Macronutrients in the Diet

Macronutrients (fats, proteins, carbohydrates)

Most calorie intake and energy comes from macronutrients or proteins, fats, and carbohydrates. The human brain is a metabolically active organ, meaning it requires a lot of energy to function. Although it takes up only 2%–3% of one's total body mass, it uses approximately 25% of the body's energy intake just while resting (Turner, 2011). This percentage increases during problem-solving tasks, while fighting fever, and in children. It is important that children receive enough daily calories from these macronutrients to fuel their growing bodies and developing brains.

	Fats	Proteins	Carbohydrates
Facts	▪ 9 calories/gram. ▪ The most concentrated source of energy. ▪ Three main types: unsaturated fats, saturated fats, and trans fats.	▪ 4 calories/gram. ▪ During digestion, proteins are broken down into amino acids. ▪ Complete proteins, are foods that contain all nine essential amino acids.	▪ 4 calories/gram. ▪ Carbohydrates are converted into glucose (sugar) during digestion. ▪ Two main types: simple and complex. ▪ To maximize health benefits, choose whole grains and fruits over processed foods and juices.
Function	▪ Fats are a carrier for fat-soluble vitamins. ▪ Unsaturated fats (primarily found in plant sources and fish) have many health benefits, including supporting good cholesterol and heart health.	▪ Protein is used to make enzymes, hormones, antibodies, and neurotransmitters. ▪ Proteins help the body build and repair tissue.	▪ Carbohydrates serve as the primary source of energy. When someone does not consume enough carbohydrates, the body attempts to use fats and proteins for energy, but these are less efficient at providing energy. ▪ Carbohydrates are also a major source of nutrient delivery.

Although macronutrients are the primary energy source for the body, micronutrients, meaning vitamins and minerals, are vital to health and development (see Figure 18). Neurobiologists and pediatricians recommend that the best way to consume all of the needed nutrients for development is through a well-balanced diet that includes plenty of fruits and vegetables, lean proteins, and complex carbohydrates, and that limits the consumption of processed foods and trans fats.

Teachers can encourage students to "eat the rainbow" by challenging them to eat as many naturally occurring different-colored foods, especially fruits and vegetables, as possible (see the edible rainbow extension activity).

NEUROANATOMICAL TIDBIT

The Blood-Brain Barrier (BBB) is a protective membrane between the blood and the central nervous system. Its primary function is to protect against pathogens entering the brain while still allowing nutrients to enter. In general, small fat-soluble molecules can pass through, but water-soluble compounds cannot, at least not without a transmitter protein (Serlin et al., 2015; Woodruff & Götz, 2018). You might think of the BBB as the bouncer at a fancy club. To extend the metaphor, transmitter proteins are the celebrity friends whom you can't get in without.

Hydration

The human brain is made of approximately 75% water, and it functions best when fully hydrated. Brain-based symptoms of dehydration include "feeling foggy" or lacking clarity, fatigue, and headaches. It's easy for students (and adults) to mistake dehydration symptoms as sickness, hunger, or fatigue. Oftentimes having a big glass of cool water can do wonders for one's overall well-being.

Water plays an essential role in delivering nutrients to the brain and also in removing toxins. In highly regimented school schedules, sometimes children do not drink enough water during their school day; this is pronounced in classrooms where water bottles or frequent water breaks are discouraged. Promote hydration in the classroom by letting students keep water bottles at their desks and encouraging them to refill them during transition times or other breaks. Students can even keep a tally chart at their desk and strive to drink three full bottles of water a day at school. Water-rich foods such as watermelon, strawberries, lettuce, celery, and cucumber can also help students stay hydrated.

FIGURE 18
Micronutrients in the Diet

Micronutrients			
Micronutrients play an essential role in health, development, and brain function.			
Vitamins		**Minerals**	
▪ Organic ▪ Fragile structure that can be broken down by heat, air, or acid (including cooking and storing)		▪ Inorganic ▪ Strong chemical structure ▪ Minerals find their way into the body through the fruits, vegetables, meats, and water consumed	
Water-Soluble	**Fat-Soluble**	**Major Minerals**	**Trace Minerals**
B Vitamins Vitamin C	Vitamin A Vitamin D Vitamin E Vitamin K	Calcium Chloride Magnesium Phosphorus Potassium Sodium Sulfur	Chromium Copper Fluoride Iodine Iron Manganese Molybdenum Selenium Zinc

Note. Information from HelpGuide (2019).

NEUROANATOMICAL TIDBIT

Located near the front of the brain, the **lamina terminalis** plays a critical role in monitoring hydration and triggering feelings of thirst. The lamina terminalis collects information about blood pressure, blood volume, nutrient consumption, and osmolar disturbances (Frank, 2019). Osmolality refers to the concentration of a solution—when a person is dehydrated, this can lead to an imbalance of sodium and water. The human body maintains a narrow range of body fluid osmolality

(Verbalis, 2007), meaning that even small changes can cause notable symptoms.

Sleep

Sleep, the "basis of the conscious experience," is essential for learning, memory, and brain function (Hobson & Pace-Schott, 2002, p. 679). School-age children require 9–12 hours of sleep a night. Neuroscientists have identified four main stages of sleep (see Figure 19).

Neuroscience studies using electroencephalogram (EEG) suggest that most dreaming, particularly vivid dreaming, occurs during REM sleep. That said, dreaming can also occur in non-REM sleep, and dreamlike states or daydreaming are present even during wakefulness (see Chapter 4). During sleep, the hippocampus overflows with information and experiences from one's waking state that are then sorted and stored into memories (Hobson & Pace-Schott, 2002). This process, called *memory consolidation*, occurs during both NREM and REM sleep (Poe et al., 2010).

Teaching students about the importance of sleep in overall health and brain development is a great opportunity to share the adverse effects of screen time at night or just before bedtime. Helping younger students form healthy habits such as limiting screen time, particularly in the 1–2 hours before bedtime, can have a lasting positive impact on their lives.

Exercise

Have you ever noticed that you were losing a class's attention and responded by giving students a quick stretching or aerobic break (e.g., jumping jacks, jumping rope, relay race, running in place, etc.)? After that exercise break, did you find that your students were more alert and able to attend the lesson at hand? This strategy was personally transformative for a restless gifted education advisory class I taught one year. Exercise increases blood flow everywhere in the body, including the brain. Increased blood flow improves brain performance.

Exercise is an essential aspect of health and wellness. The need for developing these habits in childhood has never been greater. According to the World Economic Forum, for the first time in history, the number of obese children will soon overtake the number of underweight children (Nebehay, 2017). Childhood obesity has been linked to diabetes, asthma, reduced immunity, and a host of lasting health concerns. Exercise (coupled with a well-balanced diet) can help combat childhood obesity. Although the physical benefits of exercise are well doc-

FIGURE 19
Sleep Stages

A complete sleep cycle moves through stages 1-2-3-2-1 and then stage 4. During a full night's sleep, you complete about five complete sleep cycles.

Stage 1	During the first stage of non-REM (NREM) sleep, you move from wakefulness to sleep. During this short period of light sleep, your heartbeat, breathing, and eye movements slow, and your muscles relax, sometimes twitching a bit. Your brain waves begin to slow from their daytime wakefulness patterns.
Stage 2	In the next stage of NREM sleep, your heartbeat and breathing slow further, and your muscles relax even more. This is still considered light sleep. EEGs during this stage show that brain wave activity slows but is marked by brief bursts of electrical activity (known as *sleep spindles* and *k complexes*). You spend more of your nightly sleep in Stage 2 sleep than in other sleep stages.
Stage 3	In this last stage of NREM sleep, you experience the deep restfulness needed to feel refreshed in the morning. Your heartbeat and breathing slow to their lowest levels during this stage. Your muscles are relaxed, and it may be difficult to wake you. EEGs show that brain waves become even slower (revealing delta waves).
Stage 4	REM (rapid eye movement) sleep first occurs about 90 minutes after falling asleep. Behind closed eyelids, your eyes move rapidly from side to side. Mixed frequency brain waves look similar to the patterns observed during wakefulness. Your breathing becomes faster and irregular, and your heart rate and blood pressure increase to near waking levels. In REM sleep, your arm and leg muscles become limp, which prevents you from acting out your dreams.

umented, neuroscience studies on how exercise influences cognition, learning, and attention, particularly in children, are still developing.

As neuroscience studies on the cognitive benefits of exercise in schoolchildren increase, early evidence suggests that regular exercise improves memory and processing, likely improves the health of brain cells, and may also increase brain volume in the frontal and temporal regions (Godman, 2018; Jadhav 2018).

Improved creativity, divergent thinking, and executive functioning skills have also been linked to aerobic exercise in youth (Best, 2010). Studies are also developing on the transferability of problem-solving and collaboration skills children learn while engaging in team sports and games (Best, 2010).

Additionally, exercise has been linked to improved self-confidence, reduced stress, and feeling happier. It seems that getting children in the habit of moving regularly is good not only for cardiovascular health, but also for brain health and overall well-being. The next time your class is looking tired, checked-out, or confused, taking them outside for a quick game of soccer or a walk around the track may be just the trick. (See also the "take your idea for a walk" suggestion in Chapter 4.)

Brain health and development are multivariable (Dauncey, 2012). Nutrition, hydration, sleep, exercise, and supportive learning environments all have significant and interrelated impacts on neurodevelopment. Teachers play an important role in fostering these conditions in their classrooms and encouraging these habits in their students' lives. Learning about the biological and neurobiological benefits of healthy lifestyle choices (including social and mental health) may be one of the most important lessons kids can learn in school.

KEY TERMS FOR EDUCATORS

- **Electroencephalogram (EEG):** A noninvasive procedure that records electrical activity or brain waves.

- **Memory consolidation:** The essential sorting and storing of information that occurs during NREM and REM sleep.

- **NREM sleep:** Non-rapid eye movement sleep with three stages; Stage 3 is essential for restfulness, Stage 2 is the stage with the most sleeping time, and Stage 1 transitions a person from wakefulness to sleep; along with REM sleep, NREM sleep is essential for memory consolidation.

- **Osmolality:** The concentration of a solution.

- **REM sleep:** Rapid eye movement sleep first occurs about 90 minutes after falling asleep; most dreaming, particularly vivid dreaming, occurs during REM sleep

Classroom Application

Unit Overview

In this unit, students learn specific health practices to take care of their brains. The springboard text introduces the health triangle and key concepts, including how nutrition, hydration, sleep, and wellness support brain development and function. Next, students explore some of the chemistry connections in food, including how macronutrients are broken down in the body and used by the brain. After that, students explore the four stages of NREM and REM sleep, as well as the neuroscience of why sleep is so essential to brain health and memory. Students complete an activity on hydration and the role water plays in brain function. The "make it stick" project asks students to address this unit's essential questions in a public literacy campaign.

A note of caution. Handout 8.2: Chemistry Connections in Food is about chemical reactions as they relate to the science of metabolism. Although I hope this activity encourages healthy habits, this is not a diet regimen. When teaching health in schools, teachers want to empower children to feel good about their bodies and well-being. I intentionally did not include any activities that ask students to calculate their daily calories and compare them with their peers. Learning about macro- and micronutrients lends itself to several good math extensions. However, these require both caution and a classroom culture of respect and belonging. Here are a few tips to remember:

- Healthy children come in all different shapes and sizes.
- Puberty can happen at different ages.
- Genetics plays a role in metabolism.
- Not all kids have the same access to healthy foods.

Gifted students in particular can fixate on a poorly placed comment or "overachieve" in the face of a suggested formula. Teachers want to cultivate healthy habits and happy children.

Time Suggestions

Class 1 (30 minutes)	Class 2 (45 minutes)	Class 3 (35 minutes)	Class 4 (40 minutes)	Extension (variable)
▪ Essential Questions and Learning Objectives ▪ Handout 8.1: What's Good for the Body Is Good for the Brain ▪ Brain-Based Cardio	▪ Handout 8.2: Chemistry Connections in Food*	▪ Handout 8.3: Sweet Dreams, Scholars ▪ Handout 8.4: The Well-Hydrated Brain	▪ Handout 8.5: Make It Stick!: Brain Health	▪ Extending and Transferring the Concept

*Note. This activity includes three reading comprehensions on each of the macronutrients. For engagement and comprehension, it may be best to break these up over different sessions and bring in examples of healthy options of complex carbohydrates, complete proteins, and unsaturated fats.

Name: _____ Date: _____

Keeping the Brain Healthy

Essential Questions

- What choices can you make to take better care of your brain?
- How can you be an advocate for brain health?

Learning Objectives

By the end of this lesson, I will . . .
- investigate the connections between nutrition, hydration, exercise, sleep, and brain health;
- consider how mental, physical, and social health, as well as brain and body health, are interrelated;
- research the chemical reactions that occur when macronutrients are processed by the body;
- simulate a complete sleep cycle;
- learn a fitness activity I can do to improve clarity and alertness in the classroom; and
- practice a body-brain check-in.

Name: _____ Date: _____

What's Good for the Body
Is Good for the Brain

French fries or carrot sticks? A deep breath or punching a wall? Which choices are better for your brain? Even without reviewing the latest neuroscience studies, you can probably answer those questions, but what about these?:

- A glass of water or a glass of fruit juice?
- Twenty more minutes studying math facts or going to bed 20 minutes earlier?
- A plate of fresh veggies or a plate of cooked veggies?
- A whole grain bagel or a piece of white bread?
- Lying in bed for 20 minutes if you aren't sleeping or getting up to watch a short TV show?

In this unit, we'll explore the connections between nutrition, hydration, exercise, sleep, and brain health. We will talk about how 75% of your brain is made up of water and why water is essential and generally a better choice than sugary juices. We will explore why it's always good to eat vegetables and how the vitamins in vegetables can change depending on whether they are raw or cooked. We'll also look at **macronutrients**, such as carbohydrates, and explore why complex whole gains can fuel our brains and bodies longer than simple carbohydrates. Finally, we'll study the stages of sleep and learn the importance of rest to memory formation and brain function—this is true even if you're just lying in bed in a nearly wakeful state.

Whenever we talk about health, it is important that we consider access. Not everyone has the same access to nutritious foods, clean water, healthcare, and safe, healthy environments. For example, when we explore the importance of nutritious foods, we also need to look at how **food insecurity** impacts children in our community and what we can do to make a difference on this issue. Health issues are complex, requiring the attention of scientists, activists, friends, and scholars—just like you.

When we talk about health we are talking about our overall mental, physical, and social well-being. This is also called the **health triangle**. The health triangle also applies when we talk about brain health. In fact, if something is good for the body, it's good for the brain, too. Key factors of quality brain health are nutrition, hydration, sleep, exercise/fitness, supportive and challenging learning environments, and feelings of belonging/connectedness. By the end of this unit, you should have some great self-care strategies for your brain.

HANDOUT 8.1, *continued*

Comprehension and Reflection Questions

1. What do you think the author means by "If something is good for the body, it's good for the brain"? What examples can you think of?

   _____

   _____

   _____

   _____

2. The health triangle illustrates how our physical, social, and mental health are interconnected. This unit focuses mostly on physical health. What have you already learned about mental and social health? (Hint: You might especially think back to lessons on social cognition and emotional regulation.)

   _____

   _____

   _____

   _____

3. The article says that "supportive and challenging learning environments" are important for brain health. What do you think a supportive and challenging learning environment looks like? You might think of this as your ideal classroom.

   _____

   _____

   _____

   _____

4. Being a good scientist is about asking interesting questions that matter for our communities. In what ways has science made a positive difference in our world? How can we use what we've learned about neuroscience to continue to make a positive difference?

   _____

   _____

   _____

   _____

Keeping the Brain Healthy

Brain-Based Cardio

Using a regular deck of cards, students will generate cardio challenges to complete in this fun and simple game.

Rules of Play

- Four cards per player = 1 game (in four rounds). Each player will have different exercises to complete in this 4-minute game.
- Ask if anyone has drawn a joker or other wild card. If so, everyone will join the dance party at the end of the game. Special rules if a joker or wild card is drawn:
  - If a joker or wild card has been drawn, the student(s) with that special card(s) may sit out the round and consider (or discuss) what song the class will use for the dance party.
  - If a joker or wild card is drawn, the dance party follows Round 4. If a joker or wild card was not drawn, Round 4 proceeds like the previous rounds.

- For Round 1, everyone should select one of their four cards. The teacher will set the timer for 1 minute for students to complete their unique challenge (see the Card Challenges table).
- Complete this process for Rounds 2 and 3.
- Everyone who successfully completes their card challenge wins. This game isn't about winning; it's about increasing blood flow to the brain and finding the fun in doing aerobic exercise together.
- Embrace fun and togetherness. This is a rule.
- Once students learn this game, anyone can call for a round of brain-based cardio so long as it has been at least 2 hours since the last round. The teacher can call for brain-based cardio *anytime*.
- **Variation:** It may help to have all players sort their cards into suits and call out hearts, then spades, and so forth during the game. If someone gets a break, their role is to encourage others.

Card Challenges

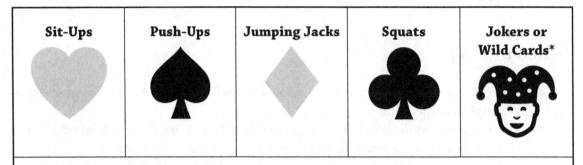

Sit-Ups	Push-Ups	Jumping Jacks	Squats	Jokers or Wild Cards*

Ace–10 = Face value × 3

For example, if you draw a 3 of hearts, you would need to do 9 sit-ups (3 × 3).

Face Cards = As many of the exercise as possible in 1 minute

For example, if you draw the queen of spades, you would need to do as many squats as possible in 1 minute.

*Note. If a player draws these cards, *all players* dance for 2 minutes to the song of the card drawer's choice after Round 4. If multiple players draw this card, use "rock, paper, scissors" between wild card drawers to determine the song choice. Everyone still dances.

HANDOUT 8.2
Chemistry Connections in Food

A **chemical reaction** occurs when a substance is converted (or changed) into another substance. Our bodies and brains process food and nutrition through a series of chemical reactions called **metabolism**.

Our brain gets most of its energy from three **macronutrients**: carbohydrates, fats, and proteins. Each is processed differently, and each is essential for brain development and function.

Carbohydrates	
	Carbohydrates include the sugars, fibers, and starches in foods like grains, fruits, corn, beans, potatoes, and rice. About half of your calories should come from carbohydrates.
Chemical Reaction 	The body changes most carbohydrates into a sugar called **glucose**. Glucose is the main energy source for cells. Because the human brain is densely concentrated with neurons (or nerve cells), the brain requires a significant amount of the glucose in your bloodstream. Approximately half of the sugar energy in your body goes to support brain function and development. There are two main categories of carbohydrates—simple and complex. **Simple carbs** contain only one or two sugars and are simpler for the body to process. Candies, soda, syrup, and white bread are examples. Filling up on these kinds of carbs can lead to spikes in blood sugar and potential weight gain. **Complex carbs** contain three or more sugars and are more complex for the body to process, meaning they give you energy longer. These include beans, peanuts, potatoes, corn, and whole grains.
Brain Function 	Appropriate and steady glucose levels help support thinking, memory, and learning. Without glucose (or access to enough glucose), the brain cannot produce neurotransmitters. Neuroscientists have shown that more complex thinking tasks require more glucose.
Interesting Facts 	Too much glucose can also be dangerous to your health. The best choice is to keep your blood sugar levels as steady as possible, with regular healthy meals and snacks. This will also help your brain work at top performance.

HANDOUT 8.2, *continued*

Comprehension and Reflection Questions

1. What is the main chemical reaction that occurs when the body processes carbohydrates?

   _____

   _____

   _____

   _____

2. What is the difference between simple and complex carbohydrates?

   _____

   _____

   _____

   _____

3. Why are carbohydrates important for brain function and development?

   _____

   _____

   _____

   _____

4. Which complex carbohydrates will you choose to fuel your body and brain?

   _____

   _____

   _____

   _____

5. Which simple carbohydrates do you like for a special treat?

   _____

   _____

   _____

   _____

Keeping the Brain Healthy

Name: _____   Date: _____

Proteins	
	Proteins include meat, poultry, seafood, beans, eggs, soy products, nuts, and seeds. School-age scholars like you need about 1 gram of protein for every 1 kg (2.2 lbs) of body mass each day.
Chemical Reaction 	When proteins are digested, they are broken down into their amino acids. Amino acids are held together by **peptide bonds**. Peptide bonds are broken up through a process called **hydrolysis**. The prefix *hydro* means "water." Hydrolysis uses the water in your body to break down food into its different parts. In this case hydrolysis uses water to break down proteins into amino acids.
Brain and Body Function 	Amino acids from proteins help the body build and repair tissue. They strengthen the immune system and help you stay full. When it comes to brain function, protein is very important. Amino acids are used to make enzymes, hormones, antibodies, and neurotransmitters. This means protein plays a direct role in chemical communication across the brain and body, including how able you are to pay attention in class, solve problems, and learn and remember new things.
Interesting Facts 	After water, proteins make up most of your body weight. There are **nine essential amino acids** that you can only get through the foods you eat. These are histidine, isoleucine, leucine, lysine, methionine, phenylalanine, threonine, tryptophan, and valine. Foods that contain all of these essential amino acids are called **complete proteins**. Examples include meat, dairy, and quinoa. Some proteins are high in fat; in general, leaner options are the healthiest choices.

Keeping the Brain Healthy

Name: _____ Date: _____

Comprehension and Reflection Questions

1. What is the role of *hydrolysis* in protein digestion? _____

_____

_____

_____

2. List three significant functions that protein helps support in the body or brain.

_____

_____

_____

_____

3. What protein do you like to eat at breakfast? _____

_____

_____

_____

4. What protein do you like to eat at lunch? _____

_____

_____

_____

5. What protein do you like to eat at dinner? _____

_____

_____

_____

Keeping the Brain Healthy

Brain-Based Learning With Gifted Students © Prufrock Press Inc.

HANDOUT 8.2, *continued*

Fats
 There are three main types of fats: **unsaturated**, **saturated**, and **trans**. In general, you want to consume more unsaturated fats than saturated or trans fats. Some foods that are higher in unsaturated fats include avocados, olive oil, peanut butter, fatty fish (such as salmon), nuts, and seeds. About a third of your daily calories should come from fats, preferably unsaturated fats.
Chemical Reaction    Fats are digested more efficiently than any other macronutrient. This means when you eat fatty foods, very little energy is used to process them. Fats are broken down by an enzyme called **lipases**. We have lipases in our mouths, stomachs, and pancreas. The **bile** (a complex salty substance) in our bodies helps thin fats, making them easier to process. Most fat processing happens in the small intestine. When a molecule of fat is completely digested it is converted to **chylomicrons**, which look like small milky globs.
Brain and Body Function    The brain is the fattiest organ in the human body. It is about 60% fat. Vitamins A, D, E, and K all require fats to be absorbed by the body. These vitamins are called fat-soluble, because they need fat as a carrier in the body. Unsaturated fats (which are primarily found in plant sources and fish) support cardio or heart health. Both unsaturated and saturated fats (in moderation) have also been linked to improved memory and learning.
Interesting Facts    Fats are the most concentrated source of energy, at 9 calories/gram. (Proteins and carbohydrates have 4 calories/gram.) Unsaturated fats are liquid at room temperature and sometimes called "oil fats" or "healthy fats." Saturated fats are solid at room temperature and are therefore sometimes called "solid fats." Trans fats are semi-solid at room temperature. These occur naturally in trace amounts in some meats and can also be produced through a process called **hydrogenation**.

Keeping the Brain Healthy

HANDOUT 8.2, *continued*

Comprehension and Reflection Questions

1. Which of the following types of fats—saturated fats, unsaturated fats, trans fats—has the most health benefits? Support your answer.

    _____

    _____

    _____

    _____

2. Besides health benefits, what are the differences between the three types of fats?

    _____

    _____

    _____

    _____

3. How do lipases and bile help our bodies process fats? _____

    _____

    _____

    _____

4. List three significant functions that fat helps support in the body or brain.

    _____

    _____

    _____

    _____

5. Which unsaturated fat do you want to try next? _____

    _____

    _____

    _____

Keeping the Brain Healthy

Name: _____ Date: _____

Sweet Dreams, Scholars

Neuroscientists have identified four main stages of sleep, outlined in the following chart. A complete sleep cycle moves through stages 1-2-3-2-1 and then stage 4. During a full night's sleep you complete about 5 complete sleep cycles.

Directions: Act out the sleep stages in the order they happen during your nighttime rest.

Sleep Stage	Definition	Acting Instructions
Stage 1	During the first stage of **non-REM (NREM)** sleep, you move from wakefulness to sleep. Your brain waves begin to slow from their daytime wakefulness patterns.	This is a short period of light sleep. During this stage, your heartbeat, breathing, and eye movements slow, and your muscles relax, sometimes twitching a bit. *Close your eyes, begin to relax, allow your muscles to twitch gently.*
Stage 2	In the next stage of NREM sleep, your brain wave activity slows but is marked by brief bursts of electrical activity (known as **sleep spindles** and **k complexes**). You spend more of your nightly sleep in Stage 2 sleep than in other sleep stage.	During this stage, your heartbeat and breathing slow further, and your muscles relax even more. Based on the sequence of sleep cycles, you spend more time in this stage than any other. *Keeping your eyes closed, relax further, calm your body.*
Stage 3	In this last stage of NREM sleep, you experience the deep restfulness needed to feel refreshed in the morning. Your brain waves become even slower (revealing **delta waves**).	During this stage, your heartbeat and breathing slow to their lowest levels during this stage. Your muscles are relaxed, and it may be difficult to wake you. *Relax further. Make your arms and legs heavy, feel your body sinking into the floor.* *Keep your eyes closed. Just as you do while sleeping at night, we will repeat Stages 2 and 1 in reverse before moving into Stage 4: REM sleep.*

HANDOUT 8.3, *continued*

Sleep Stage	Definition	Acting Instructions
Stage 4	**Rapid eye movement (REM)** sleep first occurs about 90 minutes after falling asleep. Behind closed eyelids, your eyes move rapidly from side to side. Mixed frequency brain waves look similar to the patterns observed during wakefulness.	During this stage, your breathing becomes faster and irregular, and your heart rate and blood pressure increase to near waking levels. In REM sleep, your arm and leg muscles become limp, which prevents you from acting out your dreams. *You are now deeply asleep. Your body is heavy and limp. If your teacher came by and lifted your arm it would fall back to the floor. Your breathing may be irregular as you dream.*

Getting enough sleep is very important for your growth and development, including your brain health. While you sleep, your hippocampus overflows with information from when you were awake. This information is then sorted and stored into memories. Although everyone's sleep needs are slightly different, pediatricians recommend that you need between 8 and 12 hours of sleep every night. Limiting screen time, particularly in the 1–2 hours before bedtime, can also help facilitate better sleep.

Note. Information from National Institute of Neurological Disorders and Stroke (2019).

Keeping the Brain Healthy

Name: _____ Date: _____

The Well-Hydrated Brain

Quick question: What do these four things have in common?

- Strawberries
- Celery
- Cucumbers
- The human brain

The answer might surprise you—they are all made of water. Why is water important to the human brain? Let's do a body-brain check-in.

HOW ARE YOU FEELING?
What emotions are you having? How is your head? How is your stomach? Do you feel any tension or tightness?

HOW IS YOUR CONCENTRATION?
Are you feeling alert and full of curiosity? Are you feeling bored? Is something distracting you?

HOW IS YOUR ENERGY?
Are you on the edge of your seat? Are you ready for a fitness break? Are you hungry or thirsty? Are you ready for a nap?

WHAT DO YOU NEED RIGHT NOW?
Do you need a hug, a break, a challenge question, a chance to share your thoughts, a snack, a big glass of cold water, or an opportunity to stretch?

Our bodies and brains do a good job of telling us what we need. However, the signals only work if we listen. Check in throughout the day!

After checking in, try drinking a big glass of cold water. Are you feeling any different? Do you feel better or the same? A big glass of cold water is almost always a good idea. When you are dehydrated, you can feel foggy, sleepy, and even get a headache. It's also harder to concentrate.

Water plays a very important role in keeping your brain healthy. It brings nutrients to the brain and also removes toxins. The brain insists on being well-hydrated. As soon as the water volume drops in your body, a structure called the **lamina terminalis** starts sending thirst signals. Sometimes your school days are so full that you miss these signals. By the time you feel thirsty (or notice your thirst), you're already a little dehydrated.

Adding more brain-body check-ins and more big glasses (or bottles) of water to your day can make a world of difference.

Keeping the Brain Healthy

HANDOUT 8.5

Make It Stick!: Brain Health

At the beginning of this lesson, you learned that being a good scientist is about asking questions that matter for your community. Now that you are reaching the end of this unit, how will you use what you have learned about neuroscience to continue to make a positive difference? Let's look at food insecurity as an example.

Food insecurity and hunger are pressing local and global issues in our communities. Feeding America, a leading organization in addressing hunger in the U.S., described food insecurity as "a household's inability to provide enough food for every person to live an active, healthy life." In the U.S., 1 in 9 people currently struggle with hunger.

The United Nations, the leading humanitarian group in the world, has called for a Zero Hunger goal. The UN reported that more than 820 million people were undernourished in 2017.

Not having access to the **macronutrients** as well as **micronutrients** (vitamins and minerals) causes significant health issues and hinders brain devel-

> **KEY TERMS**
>
> **Health triangle:** The relationship between our mental, physical, and social well-being.
>
> **Chemical reaction:** The process by which a substance is converted (or changed) into another substance.
>
> **Metabolism:** The way our bodies and our brains process food and nutrition. Metabolism is a series of chemical reactions that occur during digestion.
>
> **Macronutrients:** The food sources where the brain gets most of its energy. The three macronutrients in our diets are carbohydrates, fats, and proteins.
>
> **Carbohydrates:** The sugars, fibers, and starches in foods like grains, fruits, corn, beans, potatoes, and rice. The body changes most carbohydrates into a sugar called *glucose*, the main energy source for cells. About half of your calories should come from carbohydrates, preferably complex carbohydrates.
>
> **Proteins:** Meat, poultry, seafood, beans, eggs, soy products, nuts, and seeds. Proteins are made of amino acids, which are essential to build and repair tissue, strengthen the immune system, and make enzymes, hormones, antibodies, and neurotransmitters. School-age scholars like you need about 1 gram of protein for every 1 kg (2.2 lbs) of body mass each day.

opment. Addressing food insecurity and reaching the Zero Hunger goal requires leaders around the world, including student leaders like you, to advocate for access. Food insecurity is a complex issue. Understanding this issue can help you make important connections between access to resources and health outcomes for the body and brain. Resources include nutritious food, clean water, safe sleeping conditions, and supportive learning environments.

Keeping the Brain Healthy

HANDOUT 8.5, *continued*

Challenge: Public Literacy Campaign for Brain Health

You will develop a public literacy campaign for brain health focusing on these topics:

- nutrition,
- exercise,
- sleep, and
- hydration.

Address one or both of the following essential questions:

- What choices can you make to take better care of your brain?
- How can you be an advocate for brain health?

Choose your platform:

- vending machine,
- cafeteria,
- school restroom,
- hallway, or
- other places where you or others will see these reminders frequently.

> ### KEY TERMS, *continued*
>
> **Hydrolysis:** The way water molecules can break down substances into smaller parts. We learned about hydrolysis through protein digestion.
>
> **Fats:** There are three main types of fats: unsaturated, saturated, and trans. In general, you want to consume more unsaturated fats than saturated or trans fats. Other anatomical vocabulary we learned in studying how fats are digested include: lipases, bile, and chylomicrons.
>
> **Sleep cycle:** Neuroscientists have identified four main stages in a sleep cycle. Three are during non-rapid eye movement sleep (NREM), and one occurs during rapid eye movement sleep (REM). During a full night's sleep you complete about five complete sleep cycles. Sleep is essential for memory and overall health and well-being.
>
> **Lamina terminalis:** The brain structure that sends out thirst signals.
>
> **Brain and body check-in:** A quick process to listen to your brain and body signals and assess what you need in the present moment.
>
> **Food security:** A household's ability to provide enough food for every person to live an active, healthy life.

Share scientific information to spread awareness, encourage action, and change habits. Posters, editorials, and flyers work well for this public literacy project.

References

Feeding America. (2020). *How do you measure hunger?* https://www.feedingamerica.org/hunger-in-america/food-insecurity

United Nations. (n.d.). *Goal 2: Zero hunger.* https://www.un.org/sustainabledevelopment/hunger

Keeping the Brain Healthy

Extending and Transferring the Concept

This unit introduces students to several important health concepts. It also offers an introduction to issues of access and to thinking about science as a vehicle for public good. All of these themes and concepts offer opportunities for extension. The following are a few suggestions for ways you might deepen learning around these concepts in your classroom.

Handout 8.1: What's Good for the Body Is Good for the Brain

- **Would your brain rather . . . ?:** Students love to play "Would you rather?", a game in which two options are presented and they have to choose one to defend. Sometimes both alternatives are positive. Sometimes both are negative or even outrageous. The opening reading sets students up for a brain-based version of the game, in which students propose two options and then have to use their knowledge of neuroscience to defend their choice.
- **The health triangle:** Students have been exploring components of the health triangle as well as interrelations within the health triangle. Create a large health triangle in your classroom and have students post what they have learned about social, mental, and physical health on the community display.
- **How can science be used to help make the world a better place?:** Throughout this unit, center access and advocacy by asking students to wrestle with this question and propose answers and solutions. You might post this question at one of your extension centers or on a community bulletin board and give students space to offer their ideas throughout the unit. These answers could be a catalyst for powerful student-led service projects.

Brain-Based Cardio

- **Checking pulses:** Students may take their pulse on either their arm or neck. It can be tricky for students to find their pulse. Before you start the brain-based cardio game, see if students can find their pulse and take a "starting pulse." You can time students for 15 seconds and then multiply by 4 for beats per minute. After the brain-based cardio break, ask students to take their pulse again and discuss the difference. Hopefully their rate has increased. Have a conversation about what this means for the heart and the brain. Remember, brains function better with increased blood flow.

- **Teach brain-based cardio across classes:** Brain-based cardio is a simple activity that all teachers in the school can learn and offer to students. Play it at your next faculty meeting and make it available as a kinesthetic options across classes.

Handout 8.2: Chemistry Connections in Food

- **Tasting party:** Invite your class to bring in complex carbohydrates, vitamin and mineral-rich fruits and vegetables, complete proteins, and unsaturated fats, and have a tasting party. Remember, families have uneven access to healthy foods to share. If available, this may also be an activity that a Parent Teacher Association could help with. During the meal, encourage students to find a new healthy food they love. As you eat, talk about the process that is happening in your bodies to process these foods and why this matters for brain health.

- **Edible rainbow:** Another spin on this activity is to create an edible rainbow of healthy food options. This also makes a nice bulletin board or cafeteria display. To extend the health and science connections, students can label the display with nutritional information.

- **Micronutrients:** Have students explore one micronutrient a week to learn how vitamins and minerals are absorbed by the body. In addition to the health benefits of exploring this content, there is also great potential for deepening young scholars' understanding of chemistry. Invite a chemistry teacher or chemist to visit your class to share about the different structures of vitamins (fragile) and minerals (strong). See Figure 18 for a list of micronutrients. You could assign students (either individually or in small groups) a specific vitamin or mineral to research. They can share what the vitamin or mineral is, where it is found naturally, how much should be consumed daily, and what function it plays in brain and body function and development. See Figure 20 for a sample reading comprehension text on iodine. After all micronutrients have been researched, students could then work in new groups to talk about the interactions between micronutrients.

FIGURE 20
Sample Extension Text

Iodine: The Purple Mineral

Iodine is a chemical element. When you melt it, it forms a deep purple liquid. When you boil it, it transforms into a purple gas. Iodine is a halogen (meaning it is salt-producing).

Trace amounts of iodine can be found throughout our environment in water, soil, rocks, plants, animals, and humans. The Earth's largest reserve of iodine is our seawater.

Iodine is responsible for the production of the thyroid hormones, which are essential for brain and central nervous system development.

We can get our recommended daily intake of iodine by eating fish, dairy, and enriched grains. Fruits and vegetables may also contain iodine if they were grown in iodine-rich soil. Iodized salt is another source of iodine that is particularly accessible in the U.S.

Note. Information from the National Institutes of Health (2020).

Handout 8.3: Sweet Dreams, Scholars

- **EEG lesson:** Engage in class research or invite a guest expert to teach students about EEGs and to show what sleep spindles, k complexes, and delta waves look like. Some students may have had an EEG test and may be willing to share their experiences with the class.

Handout 8.4: The Well-Hydrated Brain

- **Smart water bottle:** Decorate reusable water bottles with stickers and labels with facts on the importance of hydration and access to clean water. Students can also make these water bottles for younger students or others in their community.
- **Hydration data:** Encourage students to keep their "smart water bottles" at their desks and hold each other accountable for drinking plenty of water throughout the school day. Help students track their water consumption for a week and cross-check it with data from their corresponding brain and body check-ins.

Conclusion

Congratulations to you and your students for your deep engagement with neuroscience content! I hope the text and activities in this book challenged you, sparked curiosity, and caused you to ask new questions. As you reach the end of this book, take some time to reflect and synthesize what you have learned about brain-based learning and how those lessons might impact your teaching. Likewise, give your students this same space to reflect on and synthesize what they have learned about the brain in general, their unique brains in particular, and the important role science has in creating positive change.

I recommend marking the completion of this study with a public learning event hosted by your class. The following is a recap of the essential questions, themes, big ideas in science, and key concepts explored in this book. Ask students to spend some time with this list and design an independent project they want to pursue and present at a culminating event.

Continuing to draw on the NAGC 2019 Pre-K–Grade-12 Gifted Programming Standards. These projects should require students to demonstrate an understanding of how they learn, reveal cognitive growth, and require independent investigation and research. See the NAGC Programming Standards Alignment section for some key standards to help you guide students in putting this project together.

In addition to showcasing the artifacts that students created throughout their studies, particularly their "make it stick" projects, students should also use this opportunity to prepare a unique independent project. This project may address one or more of the essential questions students found most meaningful. Students may present a research poster, PowerPoint, paper, flyer, skit, or other presentation of their choosing. Choice and creativity are actively encouraged!

Concept Review

Essential Questions

- How can learning about the key structures of the human brain help you become a better learner?
- How can you use questions as a tool for inquiry?
- How are metacognition and learning connected?
- How can you respond to the world with both wonder and reason?
- How can learning about social cognition help you approach others with empathy?
- What factors influence your developing brain? How can you use this information to grow as a problem solver?
- How are your emotions, behaviors, and thoughts connected? What does this connection look like in the brain?
- What choices can you make to take better care of your brain?
- How can you be an advocate for brain health?

Themes

- Empathy
- Curiosity
- Metacognition
- Brain plasticity
- Brain function

Big Ideas in Science

- Patterns
- Cause and Effect

- Structure and Function
- Stability and Change
- Interdependence

Neuroscience Concepts

- Brain Anatomy 101
- Interrogative Inquiry
- Maximizing Metacognitive Moments
- Sparking Connection With Wonder
- Social Cognition
- Neuroplasticity
- Emotional Regulation
- Keeping the Brain Healthy

References

Acharya, S., & Shukla, S. (2012). Mirror neurons: Enigma of the metaphysical modular brain. *Journal of Natural Science, Biology, and Medicine, 3*(2), 118–124. https://doi.org/10.4103/0976-9668.101878

Adolphs, R. (2009). The social brain: Neural basis of social knowledge. *Annual Review of Psychology, 60,* 693–716. https://doi.org/10.1146/annurev.psych.60.110707.163514

American Academy of Pediatrics & Food Research and Action Center. (2017). *Addressing food insecurity: A toolkit for pediatricians.* https://frac.org/aaptoolkit

Anderson, L., & Krathwohl, D. R. (Eds.). (2001). *A taxonomy for learning, teaching, and assessing: A revision of Bloom's taxonomy of educational objectives* (Complete ed.). Longman.

Arguinchona, J. H., & Tadi, P. (2020). Neuroanatomy, reticular activating system. *StatPearls [Internet].* https://www.ncbi.nlm.nih.gov/books/NBK549835

Ashwal, S. (2017). Disorders of consciousness in children. In K. F. Swaiman, S. Ashwal, D. M. Ferriero, N. F. Schor, R. S. Finkel, A. L. Gropman, P. L. Pearl, & M. I. Shevell (Eds.), *Swaiman's pediatric neurology* (6th ed., pp. 767–780). Elsevier.

Best, J. R. (2010). Effects of physical activity on children's executive function: Contributions of experimental research on aerobic exercise. *Developmental Review, 30*(4), 331–351. https://doi.org/10.1016/j.dr.2010.08.001

Bloom, B. (Ed.). (1956). *Taxonomy of educational objectives: The classification of educational goals. Handbook I: Cognitive domain.* Longmans Green.

Bryan, J., Osendarp, S., Hughes, D., Calvaresi, E., Baghurst, K., & Van Klinken, J. W. (2004). Nutrients for cognitive development in school-aged children. *Nutrition Reviews, 62*(8), 295–306. https://doi.org/10.1111/j.1753-4887.2004.tb00055.x

Callard, F., Smallwood, J., & Margulies, D. S. (2012). Default positions: How neuroscience's historical legacy has hampered investigation of the resting mind. *Frontiers in Psychology, 3,* 321. https://doi.org/10.3389/fpsyg.2012.00321

Carraway, K. (2014). *Transforming your teaching: Practical classroom strategies informed by cognitive neuroscience.* Norton.

Cherry, K. (2019). *How experience changes brain plasticity.* Verywell Mind. https://www.verywellmind.com/what-is-brain-plasticity-2794886

Chick, N. (2019). *Metacognition.* Vanderbilt University, Center for Teaching. https://cft.vanderbilt.edu/guides-sub-pages/metacognition

Coxon, S. (2018). Curiosity for all. In J. Danielian, E. Fogarty, & C. M. Fugate (Eds.), *Teaching gifted children: Success strategies for teaching high-ability learners* (pp. 283–286). Prufrock Press.

Dauncey, M. J. (2012). Recent advances in nutrition, genes and brain health. *Proceedings of the Nutrition Society, 71*(4), 581–591. https://doi.org/10.1017/s0029665112000237

Docter, P. (Director). (2015). *Inside out* [Film]. Pixar Studios.

Doidge, N. (2016). *The brain's way of healing: Remarkable discoveries and recoveries from the frontiers of neuroplasticity.* Penguin.

Duckworth, A. L., Kirby, T., Gollwitzer, A., & Oettingen, G. (2013). From fantasy to action: Mental contrasting with implementation intentions (MCII) improves academic performance in children. *Social Psychological and Personality Science, 4*(6), 745–753. https://doi.org/10.1177/1948550613476307

Dunst, B., Benedek, M., Jauk, E., Bergner, S., Koschutnig, K., Sommer, M., Ischebeck, A., Spinath, B. Arendasy, M., Buhner, M. Freudenthaler, H., & Neubauer, A. C. (2014). Neural efficiency as a function of task demands. *Intelligence, 42,* 22–30. https://doi.org/10.1016/j.intell.2013.09.005

Dweck, C. (2015). Carol Dweck revisits the growth mindset. *Education Week, 35*(5), 20–24.

Dweck, C. S. (2016). *Mindset: The new psychology of success.* Ballantine Books. (Original work published 2006)

Ekman, P. (1992). An argument for basic emotions. *Cognition and Emotion, 6*(3–4), 169–200. https://doi.org/10.1080/02699939208411068

Euston, D. R., Gruber, A. J., & McNaughton, B. L. (2012). The role of the medial prefrontal cortex in memory and decision making. *Neuron, 76*(6), 1057–1070. https://doi.org/10.1016/j.neuron.2012.12.002

Fadel, C., Bialik, M., & Trilling, B. (2015). *Four-dimensional education: The competencies learners need to succeed*. Center for Curriculum Redesign.

Ferguson, S. A. K. (2006, Winter). A case for affective education: Addressing the social and emotional needs of gifted students in the classroom. *Virginia Association for the Gifted Newsletter*, 1–3.

Fiedler, E. (1999). Gifted children: The promise of potential/the problems of potential. In V. L. Schwean & D. H. Saklofske (Eds.), *Handbook of psychosocial characteristics of exceptional children* (pp. 401–441). Plenum.

Fishman-Weaver, K. (2018). *Wholehearted teaching of gifted young women: Cultivating courage, connection, and self-care in schools*. Prufrock Press.

Fishman-Weaver, K. (2019). *When your child learns differently: A family approach for navigating special education services with love and high expectations*. Prufrock Press.

Flook, L., Goldberg, S. B., Pinger, L., & Davidson, R. J. (2015). Promoting prosocial behavior and self-regulatory skills in preschool children through a mindfulness-based kindness curriculum. *Developmental Psychology, 51*(1), 44–51. https://doi.org/10.1037/a0038256

Frank, M. (2019). The neuroscience of thirst: How your brain tells you to look for water. *Harvard University, Science in the News*. http://sitn.hms.harvard.edu/flash/2019/neuroscience-thirst-brain-tells-look-water

Frith, C. D., & Frith, U. (2007). Social cognition in humans. *Current Biology, 17*(16), R724–R732. https://doi.org/10.1016/j.cub.2007.05.068

Fuglestad, A. J., Rao, R., Georgieff, M. K., & Code, M. M. (2008). The role of nutrition in cognitive development. In C. A. Nelson & M. Luciana (Eds.), *Handbook of developmental cognitive neuroscience* (2nd ed., pp. 623–641). MIT Press. https://doi.org/10.7551/mitpress/7437.003.0046

Fuster, J. M. (2001). The prefrontal cortex—an update: Time is of the essence. *Neuron, 30*(2), 319–333. https://doi.org/10.1016/s0896-6273(01)00285-9

Gelb, M. J. (2004). *How to think like Leonardo da Vinci: Seven steps to genius every day*. Dell.

Gilligan, C. (1982). *In a different voice: Psychological theory and women's development*. Harvard University Press.

Gilligan, C., Ward, J., & Taylor, J. (with Bardige, B.) (Eds.). (1988). *Mapping the moral domain: A contribution of women's thinking to psychological theory and education*. Harvard University Press.

Godman, H. (2018). *Regular exercise changes the brain to improve memory and thinking skills*. Harvard Health Blog. https://www.health.harvard.edu/blog/

regular-exercise-changes-brain-improve-memory-thinking-skills-20140409
7110

Gogtay, N., & Thompson, P. M. (2010). Mapping gray matter development: Implications for typical development and vulnerability to psychopathology. *Brain and Cognition, 72*(1), 6–15. https://doi.org/10.1016/j.bandc.2009.08.009

Grossmann, T. (2013). The role of medial prefrontal cortex in early social cognition. *Frontiers in Human Neuroscience, 7,* 340. https://doi.org/10.3389/fnhum.2013.00340

Hanh, T. N. (2015). *The heart of the Buddha's teaching: Transforming suffering into peace, joy, and liberation.* Harmony. (Original work published 1999)

HelpGuide. (2019). *Vitamins and minerals.* https://www.helpguide.org/harvard/vitamins-and-minerals.htm

Hobson, J. A., & Pace-Schott, E. F. (2002). The cognitive neuroscience of sleep: Neuronal systems, consciousness and learning. *Nature Reviews Neuroscience, 3*(9), 679–693. https://doi.org/10.1038/nrn915

Hoge, R. D., & Renzulli, J. S. (1993). Exploring the link between giftedness and self-concept. *Review of Educational Research, 63*(4), 449–465. https://doi.org/10.3102/00346543063004449

Hoppe, C., & Stojanovic, J. (2009). *Giftedness and the brain.* The Psychologist. https://thepsychologist.bps.org.uk/volume-22/edition-6/giftedness-and-brain

Howard-Jones, P. (2019). *International report: Neuromyths and evidence-based practices in higher education.* Online Learning Consortium. https://olc-wordpress-assets.s3.amazonaws.com/uploads/2019/10/Neuromyths-Betts-et-al.-September-2019.pdf

Iacoboni, M. (2008). *Mirroring people: The science of empathy and how we connect with others.* Picador.

Jacobson, R. (2019). *Metacognition: How thinking about thinking can help kids.* Child Mind Institute. https://childmind.org/article/how-metacognition-can-help-kids

Jadhav, C. (2018). *Children who exercise have more brain power, finds study.* World Economic Forum. https://www.weforum.org/agenda/2018/07/children-who-exercise-have-more-brain-power-finds-study

Kerr, B. A. (1994). *Smart girls two: A new psychology of girls, women and giftedness.* Psychology Press.

Kerr, B. A., & Foley Nipcon, M. (2003). Gender and giftedness. In N. Colangelo & G. A. Davis (Eds.), *Handbook of gifted education* (3rd ed., pp. 493–506). Pearson.

Kerr, B. A., & McKay, R. (2014). *Smart girls in the 21st century: Understanding talented girls and women.* Great Potential Press.

Koch, C. (2015). *Intuition may reveal where expertise resides in the brain.* Scientific American. https://www.scientificamerican.com/article/intuition-may-reveal-where-expertise-resides-in-the-brain

Lanciego, J. L., Luquin, N., & Obeso, J. A. (2012). Functional neuroanatomy of the basal ganglia. *Cold Spring Harbor Perspectives in Medicine, 2*(12), Article a009621. https://doi.org/10.1101/cshperspect.a009621

Lovecky, D. V. (1994). Exceptionally gifted children: Different minds. *Roeper Review, 17*(2), 116–120. https://doi.org/10.1080/02783199409553637

Lovecky, D. V. (1995). Highly gifted children and peer relationships. *Counseling and Guidance Newsletter, 5*(3), 2.

Lovecky, D. V. (2011). *Exploring social and emotional aspects of giftedness in children.* Supporting Emotional Needs of the Gifted. https://sengifted.org/exploring-social-and-emotional-aspects-of-giftedness-in-children

MacFarlane, B. (2018). What is essential: Asking the essential questions. In J. Danielian, E. Fogarty, & C. M. Fugate (Eds.), *Teaching gifted children: Success strategies for teaching high-ability learners* (pp. 113–116). Prufrock Press.

Martin, R. E., & Ochsner, K. N. (2016). The neuroscience of emotion regulation development: Implications for education. *Current Opinion in Behavioral Sciences, 10,* 142–148. https://doi.org/10.1016/j.cobeha.2016.06.006

McMillan, R. L., Kaufman, S. B., & Singer, J. L. (2013). Ode to positive constructive daydreaming. *Frontiers in Psychology, 4,* 626. https://doi.org/10.3389/fpsyg.2013.00626

Medina, J. (2014). *Brain rules: 12 principles for surviving and thriving at work, home, and school* (Updated ed.). Pear Press.

Mishra, J., Merzenich, M. M., & Sagar, R. (2013). Accessible online neuroplasticity-targeted training for children with ADHD. *Child and Adolescent Psychiatry and Mental Health, 7*(1), Article 38. https://doi.org/10.1186/1753-2000-7-38

Mrazik, M., & Dombrowski, S. C. (2010). The neurobiological foundations of giftedness. *Roeper Review, 32*(4), 224–234. https://doi.org/10.1080/02783193.2010.508154

Munro, J. (2013). *High-ability learning and brain processes: How neuroscience can help us to understand how gifted and talented students learn and the implications for teaching* [Paper presentation]. ACER Research Conferences, Melbourne, Australia. https://research.acer.edu.au/research_conference/RC2013/5august/18

National Association for Gifted Children. (n.d.-a). *Identification.* https://www.nagc.org/resources-publications/gifted-education-practices/identification

National Association for Gifted Children. (n.d.-b). *Why are gifted programs needed?* https://www.nagc.org/resources-publications/gifted-education-practices/why-are-gifted-programs-needed

National Association for Gifted Children. (2019). *2019 Pre-K–Grade 12 Gifted Programming Standards.* https://www.nagc.org/sites/default/files/standards/Intro%202019%20Programming%20Standards.pdf

National Institute of Neurological Disorders and Stroke. (2019). *Brain basics: Understanding sleep.* https://www.ninds.nih.gov/Disorders/Patient-Caregiver-Education/Understanding-Sleep

National Institute of Neurological Disorders and Stroke. (2020). *Brain basics: Know your brain.* https://www.ninds.nih.gov/Disorders/Patient-Caregiver-Education/Know-Your-Brain

National Institutes of Health. (2020). *Iodine: Fact sheet for consumers.* https://ods.od.nih.gov/factsheets/Iodine-Consumer

National Scientific Council on the Developing Child. (2010). *Early experiences can alter gene expression and affect long-term development* (Working paper No. 10). Harvard University. https://developingchild.harvard.edu/resources/early-experiences-can-alter-gene-expression-and-affect-long-term-development

Nebehay, S. (2017). *The number of obese children is about to overtake the number of underweight for the first time.* World Economic Forum. https://www.weforum.org/agenda/2017/10/the-number-of-obese-children-is-about-to-overtake-the-number-of-underweight-for-the-first-time

NGSS Lead States. (2013). *Next generation science standards: For states, by states.* The National Academies Press.

The Nobel Prize. (n.d.). *Eric Kandel facts.* https://www.nobelprize.org/prizes/medicine/2000/kandel/facts

O'Boyle, M. W. (2008). Mathematically gifted children: Developmental brain characteristics and their prognosis for well-being. *Roeper Review, 30*(3), 181–186. https://doi.org/10.1080/02783190802199594

Oettingen, G. (2014). *Rethinking positive thinking: Inside the new science of motivation.* Current.

Oettingen, G., Mayer, D., Sevincer, A. T., Stephens, E. J., Pak, H.-J., & Hagenah, M. (2009). Mental contrasting and goal commitment: The mediating role of energization. *Personality and Social Psychology Bulletin, 35*(5), 608–622. https://doi.org/10.1177/0146167208330856

Okon-Singer, H., Hendler, T., Pessoa, L., & Shackman, A. J. (2015). The neurobiology of emotion–cognition interactions: Fundamental questions and strategies for future research. *Frontiers in Human Neuroscience, 9,* Article 58. https://doi.org/10.3389/fnhum.2015.00058

Payne, P., & Crane-Godreau, M. A. (2015). The preparatory set: A novel approach to understanding stress, trauma, and the bodymind therapies. *Frontiers in Human Neuroscience, 9,* Article 178. https://doi.org/10.3389/fnhum.2015.00178

Poe, G. R., Walsh, C. M., & Bjorness, T. E. (2010). Cognitive neuroscience of sleep. *Progress in Brain Research, 185,* 1–19. https://doi.org/10.1016/B978-0-444-53702-7.00001-4

Reis, S., & McCoach, D. (2002). Underachievement in gifted students. In M. Neihart, S. M. Reis, N. M. Robinson, & S. M. Moon (Eds.), *The social and emotional development of gifted children: What do we know?* (pp. 81–92). Prufrock Press.

Rimm, S. (1999). *See Jane win: The Rimm report on how 1,000 girls became successful women.* Three Rivers Press.

Robbins, A. (2006). *The overachievers: The secret lives of driven kids.* Hyperion.

Rypma, B., Berger, J. S., Prabhakaran, V., Bly, B. M., Kimberg, D. Y., Biswal, B. B., & D'Esposito, M. (2006). Neural correlates of cognitive efficiency. *NeuroImage, 33*(3), 969–979. https://doi.org/10.1016/j.neuroimage.2006.05.065

Schuler, P. (2002). Perfectionism in gifted children and adolescents. In M. Neihart, S. M. Reis, N. M. Robinson, & S. M. Moon (Eds.), *The social and emotional development of gifted children: What do we know?* (pp. 71–81). Prufrock Press.

Serlin, Y., Shelef, I., Knyazer, B., & Friedman, A. (2015). Anatomy and physiology of the blood-brain barrier. *Seminars in Cell & Developmental Biology, 38,* 2–6. https://doi.org/10.1016/j.semcdb.2015.01.002

Shabani, K., Khatib, M., & Ebadi, S. (2010). Vygotsky's zone of proximal development: Instructional implications and teachers' professional development. *English Language Teaching, 3*(4), 237–248.

Stanger-Hall, K. F. (2012). Multiple-choice exams: An obstacle for higher-level thinking in introductory science classes. *Cell Biology Education—Life Sciences Education, 11*(3), 294–306. https://doi.org/10.1187/cbe.11-11-0100

Stawarczyk, D., Majerus, S., Van der Linden, M., & D'Argembeau, A. (2012). Using the daydreaming frequency scale to investigate the relationships between mind-wandering, psychological well-being, and present-moment awareness. *Frontiers in Psychology, 3,* 363. https://doi.org/10.3389/fpsyg.2012.00363

Sousa, D. A. (2009). *How the gifted brain learns* (2nd ed.). Corwin.

Sousa, D. A. (2017). *How the brain learns* (5th ed.). Corwin.

Tetreault, N. (2019). *Neuroscience of asynchronous development in bright minds.* 2e News. https://www.2enews.com/child-development/neuroscience-of-asynchronous-development-in-bright-minds

Tibke, J. (2019). *Why the brain matters: A teacher explores neuroscience.* SAGE.

Tomasello, M. (1999). *The cultural origins of human cognition.* Harvard University Press.

Turner, J. (2011). Your brain on food: a nutrient-rich diet can protect cognitive health. *Generations: Journal of the American Society on Aging, 35*(2), 99–106.

United States Department of Agriculture. (2019). *Child nutrition programs.* https://www.ers.usda.gov/topics/food-nutrition-assistance/child-nutrition-programs

Verbalis, J. G. (2007). How does the brain sense osmolality? *Journal of the American Society of Nephrology, 18*(12), 3056–3059. https://doi.org/10.1681/ASN.2007070825

Willis, J. (2006). *Research-based strategies to ignite student learning.* Association for Supervision and Curriculum Development.

Wilson, D., & Conyers, M. (2014). *Metacognition: The gift that keeps giving.* Edutopia. https://www.edutopia.org/blog/metacognition-gift-that-keeps-giving-donna-wilson-marcus-conyers

Wilson, N. S., & Smetana, L. (2009). Questioning as thinking: A metacognitive framework. *Middle School Journal, 41*(2), 20–28.

Winton, B. J. (2013). *Reversing underachievement among gifted secondary students* [Doctoral dissertation, University of Missouri, Columbia].

Woodruff, A., & Götz, J. (2018). *What is the blood-brain barrier?* University of Queensland. https://qbi.uq.edu.au/brain/brain-anatomy/what-blood-brain-barrier

Yeh, F. C., Vettel, J. M., Singh, A., Poczos, B., Grafton, S. T., Erickson, K. I., Tseng, W.-Y. I., & Verstynen, T. D. (2016). Quantifying differences and similarities in whole-brain white matter architecture using local connectome fingerprints. *PLoS Computational Biology, 12*(11), Article e1005203. https://doi.org/10.1371/journal.pcbi.1005203

About the Author

Kathryn Fishman-Weaver, Ph.D., is an educator, author, and relentless optimist. She believes that everyone has wisdom to offer and that we can all make a positive difference. These are both lessons she learned from her students. Dr. Fishman-Weaver holds a faculty position in the University of Missouri, College of Education, where she serves as the Director of Academic Affairs and Engagement for Mizzou Academy. As a school principal she strives for wholehearted and culturally responsive leadership. This is her third book. Her previous books, *Wholehearted Teaching of Gifted Young Women: Cultivating Courage, Connection, and Self-Care in Schools* (2018) and *When Your Child Learns Differently: A Family Approach for Navigating Special Education Services With Love and High Expectations* (2019), also address her passion for engaging and relevant learning opportunities for neurodiverse students.

Dr. Fishman-Weaver lives with her family in a not-so-quiet house in the Midwest. Working on this book led to a deeper fondness for the unique and wonderful brains of her loved ones. In particular, she appreciates the aptitude they have for distracting her from "work" and getting her to pay more attention to "life."

NAGC Programming Standards Alignment

Chapters	Student Outcomes	Evidence-Based Practices
Chapter 2 Chapter 7 Chapter 8	**1.1. Self-Understanding.** Students with gifts and talents recognize their interests, strengths, and needs in cognitive, creative, social, emotional, and psychological areas.	
Chapter 1 Chapter 3 Chapter 4 Chapter 6 Chapter 8 Conclusion Project	**1.2. Self-Understanding.** Students with gifts and talents demonstrate understanding of how they learn and recognize the influences of their identities, cultures, beliefs, traditions, and values on their learning and behavior.	

Chapters	Student Outcomes	Evidence-Based Practices
Chapter 1 Chapter 5	**1.3. Self-Understanding.** Students with gifts and talents demonstrate understanding of and respect for similarities and differences between themselves and their cognitive and chronological peer groups and others in the general population.	
Chapter 6 Chapter 7 Conclusion Project	**1.5. Cognitive, Psychosocial, and Affective Growth.** Students with gifts and talents demonstrate cognitive growth and psychosocial skills that support their talent development as a result of meaningful and challenging learning activities that address their unique characteristics and needs.	
Chapter 1 Chapter 8	**3.1. Curriculum Planning.** Students with gifts and talents demonstrate academic growth commensurate with their abilities each school year.	3.1.4. Educators design differentiated curriculum that incorporates advanced, conceptually challenging, in-depth, and complex content for students with gifts and talents.
Chapter 2 Chapter 3 Chapter 5 Chapter 7	**3.2. Talent Development.** Students with gifts and talents demonstrate growth in social and emotional and psychosocial skills necessary for achievement in their domain(s) of talent and/or areas of interest.	

Chapters	Student Outcomes	Evidence-Based Practices
Conclusion Project	**3.4. Instructional Strategies.** Students with gifts and talents demonstrate their potential or level of achievement in their domain(s) of talent and/or areas of interest.	3.4.2. Educators provide opportunities for students with gifts and talents to explore, develop, or research in existing domain(s) of talent and/or in new areas of interest.
Chapter 2 Chapter 3 Chapter 4 Chapter 5 Chapter 6 Chapter 7 Chapter 8 Conclusion Project	**3.5. Instructional Strategies.** Students with gifts and talents become independent investigators.	3.5.1. Educators model and teach metacognitive models to meet the needs of students with gifts and talents such as self-assessment, goal setting, and monitoring of learning. 3.5.3. Educators scaffold independent research skills within students' domain(s) of talent.
Chapter 2 Chapter 4 Chapter 5 Chapter 6 Chapter 7 Chapter 8 Conclusion Project	**4.1. Personal Competence.** Students with gifts and talents demonstrate growth in personal competence and dispositions for exceptional academic and creative productivity. These include self-awareness, self-advocacy, self-efficacy, confidence, motivation, resilience, independence, curiosity, and risk taking.	4.1.2. Educators provide opportunities for self-exploration, development and pursuit of interests, and development of identities supportive of achievement (e.g., through mentors and role models) and a love of learning.
Chapter 5 Chapter 7 Conclusion Project	**4.2. Social Competence.** Students with gifts and talents develop social competence manifested in positive peer relationships and social interactions.	4.2.3. Educators assess and provide instruction on psychosocial and social and emotional skills needed for success in school, their community, and society.

Chapters	Student Outcomes	Evidence-Based Practices
Chapter 1 Chapter 2 Chapter 3 Chapter 4 Chapter 5 Chapter 6 Chapter 7 Chapter 8	**5.1. Comprehensiveness.** Students with gifts and talents demonstrate growth commensurate with their abilities in cognitive, social-emotional, and psychosocial areas as a result of comprehensive programming and services.	5.1.2. Educators use enrichment options to extend and deepen learning opportunities within and outside of the school setting.
Chapter 3 Chapter 5 Chapter 6 Chapter 7	**6.2. Psychosocial and Social-Emotional Development.** Students with gifts and talents develop critical psychosocial skills and show social-emotional growth as a result of educators and counselors who have participated in professional learning aligned with national standards in gifted education and Standards for Professional Learning.	
Chapter 1 Chapter 2 Chapter 3 Chapter 4 Chapter 5 Chapter 6 Chapter 7 Chapter 8	**6.4. Lifelong Learning.** Students develop their gifts and talents as a result of educators who are lifelong learners, participating in ongoing professional learning and continuing education opportunities.